CANDY
EXPERIMENTS

D0370742

LORALEE LEAVITT

**Andrews McMeel
Publishing, LLC**
Kansas City · Sydney · London

Andrews McMeel Publishing, LLC
an Andrews McMeel Universal company
1130 Walnut Street, Kansas City, Missouri 64106

www.andrewsmcmeel.com

12 13 14 15 16 SHO 10 9 8 7 6 5 4 3 2 1

ISBN: 978-1-4494-1836-6

Library of Congress Control Number: 2011944678

Design by Holly Ogden

Attention: Schools and Businesses
Andrews McMeel books are available at quantity discounts with bulk
purchase for educational, business, or sales promotional use. For information,
please e-mail the Andrews McMeel Publishing Special Sales Department:
specialsales@amuniversal.com

For my husband, who poured our first density rainbow
with steady hands.

For my children, a.k.a. lab assistants, who joined me in
smashing, melting, dissolving, smelling, braiding, stretching,
and destroying candy for the sake of science.

And especially for my oldest daughter, who put her
Nerds in water and invented candy experiments.

CONTENTS

ACKNOWLEDGMENTS

Many thanks to biochemist Michael Corey, carbohydrate chemist Jonathan Stapley, and Walter Bowyer, professor of chemistry at Hobart and William Smith Colleges, who reviewed experiments and clarified my understanding of innumerable chemical concepts.

Additional thanks to Frost Steele, associate professor in the department of Nutrition, Dietetics & Food Science at Brigham Young University, for explanations about nutrition and oil in candy; biochemist Lorin R. Thompson, for conversations about gelatin and unhappy gummi worms; Theodore J. Allen, associate professor of physics at Hobart and William Smith Colleges, for reviewing the physics of comets and cold-water currents; geology teacher Michelle Davis, for a description of the butterscotch smashing experiment and explanations of conchoidal fractures; dermatologist Katie Bassett, MD, for conversations about sunscreen and DNA; orthodontist Barton L. Soper, for explaining how sticky candy destroys braces; Dawn Motes of Dawn's Candy & Cake, for demonstrations of chocolate tempering; and Cynthia McVey, APR, of Hobart and William Smith Colleges and Cindy Lee Associates, for helping me find answers.

Thanks to my candy-experiment testers and reviewers for their careful reading and their experiment excitement.

And finally, thanks to my parents for sending me to Cougar Summer Science Camp, for putting up with my post-camp purple cabbage indicator experiments, and for photographing Diet Coke and Mentos geysers one dark summer night.

INTRODUCTION

You may think that candy is just a sugary snack. Think again.

With candy, you can become a scientific detective. Test candy for secret ingredients. Peel the skin off candy corn, or float an "m" from M&M's. Spread candy dyes into rainbows, or pour rainbow layers of colored water. Turn candy into crystals. Make enormous gummi snakes. Sink marshmallows, float taffy, or send soda spouting skyward. You can even make your own lightning.

Just try candy experiments.

EXPERIMENT tips

Wear an apron or an old T-shirt, because candy and oil can stain clothes.

Always ask a grown-up to help you heat candy in the microwave or the oven. Melted candy can get hotter than boiling water. If you touch it, you could get burned.

Never heat a jawbreaker.

Microwave times will depend on what kind of microwave you use. Always watch candy in the microwave to make sure that you don't heat it too much.

Don't eat or drink
the experiments.
Candy might have germs on it
if people have touched and
handled it, and baking soda
can make you sick
if you eat too much.

Keep wet rags
or paper towels
ready to clean up
sticky spills.

If you leave candy water
sitting around for several days,
it might grow mold.
If this happens,
throw the experiment away
and start over.

CANDY
EXPERIMENTS

Candy is made from sugar. But it also has secret ingredients that give it flavor and texture. Here's how to test for some of them.

chapter 1

SECRET INGREDIENTS

SOUR CANDY BUBBLE TEST

Time: 1 to 5 minutes

Skill Level: Easy

Acid in your stomach helps you digest your food. Acid on your teeth breaks down the enamel and causes tooth decay. Acid in lemon juice makes it taste sour. Is there acid in your candy?

A sour taste is the body's way of identifying acid. If your candy tastes sour, it contains acid. To test for acid, try this.

What you need:

Sour candy, such as Warheads, Lemonheads, Sour Skittles, sour Laffy Taffy, Sour Patch Kids or other sour gummies, or Pixy Stix

Small bowl filled with ½ cup warm water

Baking soda

What to do:

1. Drop the candy into the water. Let the sour part of the candy dissolve, such as the sour powder on gummies or the outer coating of Lemonheads. You can stir the water to help the candy dissolve faster. (If a waxy layer forms on the surface of the water, try to scrape or spoon it off.)

2. Sprinkle a spoonful of baking soda into the water.

3. Watch for bubbles. If bubbles form, there's acid in the candy.

Alternative:

For super-sour candy like Warheads, start by dissolving the baking soda in the water. Then drop in the Warheads and watch the bubbles rise.

What's happening:

When baking soda (a base) mixes with an acid, it releases carbon dioxide gas. This is what forms the bubbles. The more bubbles you see, the more acidic the candy is.

This same reaction is what makes bubbles in baked foods like crackers, cookies, and pancakes. In some food, baking soda reacts with acid in the dough. Cooks also use baking powder, a mixture of baking soda and acid that bubbles when it's wet.

Bubbles rise from acidic Warheads dropped in baking soda water.

more fun

Ever tried a fizzy Zotz candy? This kind of candy contains its own acid test. In the candy filling, acid is mixed with baking soda. When the filling gets wet, the acid reacts with the baking soda, creating fizzy bubbles.

To see Zotz in action, drop a piece into some water and watch for bubbles. For faster results, smash it first.

CAUTION: Don't eat lots of baking soda or drink lots of baking soda water. It could make your body too basic (the opposite of acidic), and you might get sick.

SOUR CANDY COLOR TEST

Time: 5 minutes (plus 1 hour to make indicator)

Skill Level: Medium

You can use color, such as the color in purple cabbage, to detect the acid in sour candy. To see the color change, try this.

What you need:

Small bowls

Purple cabbage indicator
(To make this, rip or chop enough purple cabbage to fill about 1 cup and soak it in 1 cup of hot water until the water is purple. For a darker color, boil the cabbage in water.)

Sour candy, such as Warheads, Lemonheads, SweeTARTS, or sour gummies (avoid red or pink)

What to do:

1. Fill a bowl with the cabbage indicator.
2. Add a piece of the candy and let it dissolve. You can stir the water to help the candy dissolve faster.
3. If the indicator turns pink, the candy is acidic.

What's happening:

The pigment in purple cabbage turns pink in acid. When you dissolve acidic candy, the acid changes the cabbage color to pink. (If you used red or pink candy for the experiment, you might not be able to tell if the cabbage color actually changed.)

Many kinds of candy contain acid, especially if they taste sour, like Lemonheads, Skittles, Starburst, and SweeTARTS. To find more acidic candy, check the labels for ingredients like citric acid or malic acid, or try this test with candy that tastes sour.

The cabbage indicator turns blue when you add a base. To make your candy water basic, add baking soda and watch the color change.

You can also use your purple cabbage indicator to test other household ingredients for acid, like vinegar, lemon juice, or clear soda, such as 7UP. If you have any indicator left, store it in an airtight container in the refrigerator.

Acidic Warheads turn purple cabbage indicator pink.

FLOATING OIL TEST

Time: 5 to 10 minutes

Skill Level: Easy

Many chewy candies contain a different secret ingredient: oil. Can you see the oil for yourself?

What you need:

Chewy candy containing oil, such as Starburst, Skittles, Tootsie Rolls, or taffy

Small bowl of warm water

What to do:

1. Drop the candy into the bowl of warm water. Let it start to dissolve.
2. After a few minutes, look for shiny puddles floating on the surface.
3. When the water cools, look for a white waxy layer on top.

What's happening:

Many kinds of chewy candy are made with oil, such as hydrogenated palm kernel oil. The oil keeps the candy from sticking to the machinery in the candy factory. It also helps make the candy smooth, soft, and chewy.

When you dissolve the candy in water, the hydrogenated palm kernel oil melts and forms the shiny puddles. In colder water, it can cool to a white, waxy solid. Since oil is lighter than water, it floats.

Oil spots from dissolved Skittles.

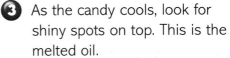

OIL SPOT TEST

Time: 5 to 20 minutes

Skill Level: Get a grown-up

Here's another way to see the oil in candy.

What you need:

Starburst or Tootsie Rolls

Microwave-safe plate

Microwave or oven

What to do:

1. Place the candy on the plate.
2. Microwave the candy until it turns liquid and bubbly, 30 seconds to 1 minute. (Alternative: Melt it in the oven at 300°F on an aluminum foil–lined baking sheet.) **Caution: hot!**

 3. As the candy cools, look for shiny spots on top. This is the melted oil.

4. When it's completely cool, the oil will harden into whitish spots. Scrape them off and rub them between your fingers to feel the oil.

What's happening:

Starburst candy contains almost 10 percent hydrogenated palm kernel oil. A Tootsie Roll contains almost 9 percent partially hydrogenated soybean oil. When you microwave the candy, the oil melts and can separate from the sugar.

Waxy spots of oil on a melted Starburst.

CHOCOLATE BLOOM

Time: Several hours to several days

Skill Level: Get a grown-up

Chocolate is made of cocoa butter, cocoa solids, and other ingredients that have been mixed together. Can you take them apart to find secret ingredients?

What you need:

Chocolate

Small heatproof plate

Heat source, such as a microwave, oven, or hair dryer

What to do:

1 Put the chocolate on the plate and heat it until it starts to melt. You can use a microwave, a low oven, a hair dryer, or even a sunny windowsill. (Chocolate melts fast. If it doesn't look melted, poke it with a fork to check.)

2 After the chocolate cools, check for light streaks. (It can take anywhere from a few hours to a few days for the streaks to form.) These streaks are made of cocoa butter.

3 If no streaks appear, melt and cool the chocolate again.

What's happening:

To build a tower, you might stack Legos in one column. Or you might make a wide tower, interlocking the Legos. If you try to knock them down, which one falls first? Which one is more stable?

Like blocks, cocoa butter molecules stack together to form structures, or crystals. Some crystals are stable—the molecules stay stacked for a long time. But other structures are not so stable.

When chocolate heats, the cocoa butter crystals break apart. Then, as the chocolate cools, the cocoa butter molecules stack back together. If they stack in an unstable formation, eventually the molecules will slide into more stable positions. As they do, some of the cocoa butter pushes out past the solid particles and forms into white crystals of pure cocoa butter. This causes the light spots and streaks, which are known as "chocolate bloom."

Chocolate makers heat and cool their chocolate with a special process called "tempering." Tempering helps form stable crystals in the chocolate, which keeps it from blooming.

Can't wait to see cocoa butter? Touch your melted chocolate with a sheet of paper. If you see a grease spot, some cocoa butter has soaked into your paper. (If melted chocolate sticks to the paper, let it cool down and then peel off the chocolate. You'll see the cocoa butter underneath.)

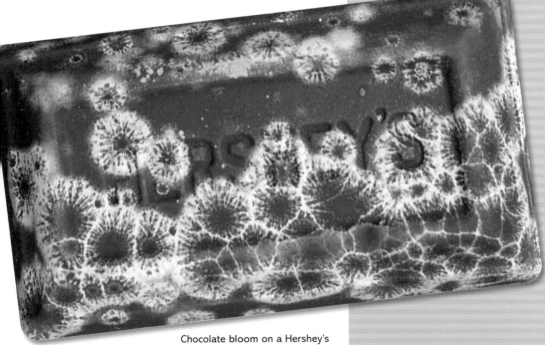

Chocolate bloom on a Hershey's chocolate bar.

SUGAR BLOOM

Time: 1 day

Skill Level: Easy

Chocolate candy contains sugar. Can you separate some sugar from the rest of the chocolate?

What you need:

Chocolate bar

Small plate

Water

What to do:

1. Put the chocolate on the plate and sprinkle a little water on it.
2. Put the wet chocolate someplace cool and dry, such as the refrigerator.
3. When the water has dried, look for a shiny sticky layer or for small white particles that resemble frost.

What's happening:

When chocolate gets wet, some of the sugar dissolves in the water. As the water dries, the sugar returns to solid form, sometimes as crystals. This can create a shiny sugar layer or a scattering of white frostlike particles, known as "sugar bloom."

Sugar crystals, or sugar bloom, on a Hershey's chocolate bar.

SKIN THE CANDY

Time: 5 minutes

Skill Level: Easy

Did you know that some candies shed their skin like snakes? They're covered in a secret ingredient that comes off in water. To see for yourself, try this.

What you need:

Candy, such as candy corn, jelly beans, Dots, Nerds, or Tootsie Rolls

Small bowl of warm water

What to do:

1. Drop the candy into the warm water.
2. Look for a waxy skin that peels off the candy.

What's happening:

Many kinds of candy are covered with a polish called "confectioner's glaze." This makes the candy shiny and keeps pieces from sticking together. The glaze is made from ingredients such as shellac, wax, vegetable oil, or starch.

When you put the candy in the water, the glaze starts to peel off. Candy companies use this experiment to check the polish and the candy covering on their products.

Candy corn losing its skin, or confectioner's glaze.

SECRET AIR BUBBLES

Time: 5 to 30 minutes

Skill Level: Easy

Taffy and other chewy candies have a secret ingredient to make them soft. You won't find it on any ingredient label, but you can see it if you put the candy in water.

What you need:

Taffy, Starburst, Tootsie Rolls, Laffy Taffy, or other soft, chewy candy

Small clear bowl of water

What to do:

1. Put the candy into the bowl of water.
2. Wait a few minutes, then check the bowl. Do you see air bubbles rising?
3. After about 30 minutes, look at the surface of the water. Do you see bubbles?

What's happening:

Have you ever seen a taffy machine in a candy store? The machine stretches and folds the candy over and over. As the taffy is folded, air bubbles get trapped inside. These air bubbles help make the candy soft. Without the air bubbles, the taffy would be as hard as a Jolly Rancher.

Air bubbles also change the color of the candy. They make it light colored and opaque (not clear). If there were no air bubbles, your taffy might be as clear as glass!

Air bubbles from dissolving taffy.

SNAP, CRACKLE, POP ROCKS

Time: 5 minutes

Skill Level: Easy

What secret ingredient makes Pop Rocks pop?

What you need:

Package of Pop Rocks

A glass of water

What to do:

1. Pour the Pop Rocks into the water.
2. Watch—and listen—for bubbles.

What's happening:

Pop Rocks are made by mixing carbon dioxide gas into melted candy. As the candy cools, the carbon dioxide is trapped in microscopic bubbles. When you put Pop Rocks in water (or your mouth), the candy dissolves, releasing the carbon dioxide with a popping sound. The carbon dioxide gas bubbles to the surface.

Why do Pop Rocks sting your tongue? Some scientists think the stinging sensation is caused by the expanding bubbles of carbon dioxide. It may also be because carbon dioxide gas tastes sour.

Air bubbles explode out of Pop Rocks.

Want to make your own bubbly dessert? Dissolve a package of Jell-O in ½ cup of boiling water, stir in 1½ cups plain seltzer water, and refrigerate. Bubbles from the carbonated water will be trapped in the Jell-O, making a dessert that tingles the tongue like Pop Rocks.

HOW MUCH "POP" IN POP ROCKS?

Time: 5 to 10 minutes

Skill Level: Medium

Pop Rocks "pop" in your mouth because they contain explosive bubbles of pressurized carbon dioxide. How much carbon dioxide is there in a package of Pop Rocks?

Once you start this experiment, you will need to move fast. Read all the steps before you start, so that you know exactly what to do.

What you need:

Plastic wrap

Clear glass filled to the very top with water

Pop Rocks

Rubber band

What to do:

 Lay plastic wrap over the glass, pressing it down against the water to remove air bubbles. Fold the plastic wrap back.

2 Dump in the Pop Rocks.

3 Immediately cover the glass with the plastic wrap, pushing down on the plastic to remove any air bubbles.

4 Wrap the rubber band around the glass to seal the plastic wrap.

 Watch the bubbles rise to the surface. The gas from the Pop Rocks will be trapped under the plastic.

What's happening:

When you dissolve the Pop Rocks, carbon dioxide gas escapes as bubbles. The bubbles are trapped under the plastic wrap, so you can see how much gas there is in Pop Rocks.

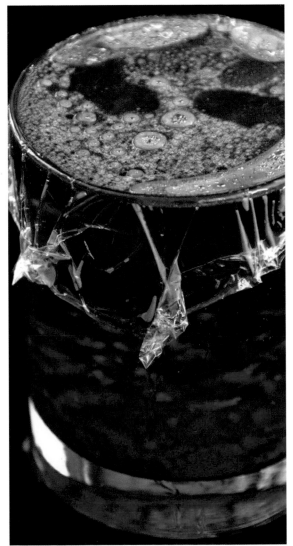

more fun

Kids used to warn each other that anyone who ate Pop Rocks and drank soda at the same time would explode. You can prove them wrong with this experiment. Dump Pop Rocks into a small bottle of soda, then fasten a balloon over the top of the soda bottle and watch it fill up with gas. Where do you think most of the gas comes from—the Pop Rocks or the soda?

Pop Rocks air bubbles trapped beneath plastic wrap.

FIND HIDDEN CANDY

Time: 5 minutes

Skill Level: Easy

Did you know that there is "hidden candy" in other foods that you eat? To find it, try this.

What you need:

Sweet food, such as cookies, soda, cereal, granola bars, or gummi fruit snacks, with ingredient label

Candy made mostly from sugar, such as mint Life Savers, Altoids, or Smarties (To check that your candy is made mostly from sugar, look at the ingredient label to see how many grams are in one serving. Then check the sugar content of a serving. If the amount of sugar is almost the same as the serving size, then your candy is made mostly from sugar.)

Kitchen scale that measures grams

What to do:

1. Check the ingredient label on your sweet food to see how much sugar one serving contains.

2. Weigh the candy on the kitchen scale, adding pieces until the weight of the candy matches the weight of the sugar. Eating one serving of your sweet food would be like eating that much candy.

What you see:

Most candy is made from sugar, corn syrup, and flavorings. These same ingredients are used to sweeten many different kinds of foods. For instance, one bottle of orange soda has 84 grams of added sugar. That's like eating 11½ rolls of Smarties or 21 mint Life Savers.

If you check ingredient labels, you'll see that some snacks are actually candy in disguise, such as gummi "fruit snacks" made of corn syrup, sugar, flavorings, and gelatin. They're really just gummi worms with a different shape.

One bottle of orange soda contains 84 grams of sugar, the weight of the candy on the scale.

Candy comes in all sorts of colors. Where did all those colors come from? How can you mix new colors? Can you unmix them?

In this chapter, you'll play with candy colors. Make your own colors with M&M's, or use chromatography to unmix colors. You can also make colored stripes, M&M's comets, and candy rainbows.

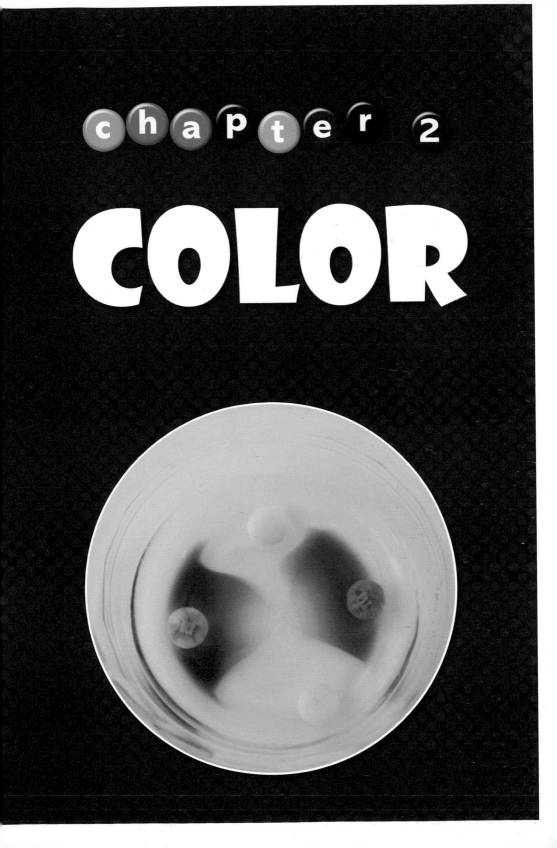

chapter 2

COLOR

MAKE YOUR OWN COLORS WITH CANDY

Time: 5 minutes

Skill Level: Easy

Ever mix puddles of paint to make new colors? Try it with candy, too!

What you need:

Red, yellow, and blue M&M's (or other colored candy, such as Skittles, jawbreakers, Jolly Ranchers, or lollipops)

Small clear or white bowl filled with about ½ cup of water

What to do:

1 Drop 2 colored M&M's into the bowl of water.

2 Wait for the sugar shell to dissolve, about 3 minutes. What color did you make?

What's happening:

Like paints, M&M's come in the primary colors of red, yellow, and blue. You can mix these colors together to make new colors. Red and yellow make orange, yellow and blue make green, and blue and red make purple.

You might have to experiment before you find color combinations you like. For instance, if your mix of red and yellow is more red than orange, add more yellow.

Red and yellow M&M's make orange.

Candy makers create candy in every color imaginable, but they all start with just a few dyes (there are nine certified colors and some nature-derived color additives approved by the U.S. Food and Drug Administration). Can you mix M&M's to create some of your favorite candy colors?

RED AND YELLOW MAKE ORANGE— OR DO THEY?

Time: 5 minutes

Skill Level: Easy

Drop 2 red M&M's and 2 yellow M&M's into a bowl of water. Do you think the colors will mix themselves together to create orange? To see what really happens, try this.

What you need:

Colored candy, such as M&M's or Skittles

Small clear or white bowl of water

What to do:

1. Drop 2 to 4 pieces of candy into the bowl of water. Do not stir.
2. Watch the pools of color spread. Do the colors combine?

What's happening:

When you put the candy in the water, the colored sugar in the candy coating starts to dissolve. The dense sugar water sinks, forming a puddle of color on the bottom and pushing the less dense water out of the way. As the candy dissolves, the puddle spreads farther.

Because the puddles spread so quickly, you might think that when two puddles meet, they'll mix right together. But they don't. This is because the two puddles have a similar density, so one can't push the other out of the way. Instead, the puddles spread sideways, pushing aside clear water until the two puddles seem to have met completely.

So do they ever mix? Water molecules are always moving, and eventually this movement will cause the colors to blur and mix together. If you want to speed up the process, just give it a good stir!

Why don't these M&M's colors mix together?

Try Everlasting Color Wars by dropping several Everlasting Gobstoppers into a bowl. Since Gobstoppers have several colored layers, new colors will keep spreading out. For some candies, the colors will spread far, while other candies will be surrounded by color, like castles under siege. Does it make any difference which colors you use, or how you place the candy?

WATERY STRIPES

Time: 5 minutes

Skill Level: Easy

Can you make colored stripes in a bowl of water? Sure you can—with striped candy.

What you need:

1 starlight mint (round striped peppermint candy)

Small clear or white bowl of water

What to do:

1. Drop the peppermint into the bowl of water. Do not stir.
2. Watch the colors dissolve into stripes on the bottom of the bowl.

What's happening:

As the candy dissolves, it forms sugar water. The sugar water is denser than regular water, so it sinks. At the bottom of the bowl, the sugar water spreads outward, but it doesn't mix right away. That's why you can still see stripes.

Since water molecules are constantly moving, eventually the colors will mix together, and the stripes will fade.

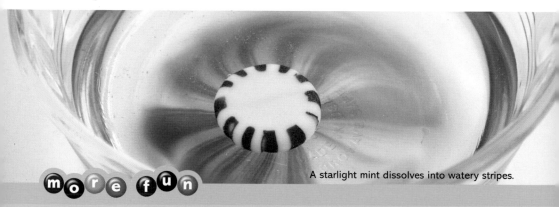

A starlight mint dissolves into watery stripes.

more fun

Try this same experiment with a candy cane. Since candy canes come in a variety of colors, you'll be able to make lots of kinds of stripes.

HALLEY'S COMET M&M'S

Time: 5 to 10 minutes

Skill Level: Medium

Can you use an ice pack to turn M&M's into comets?

What you need:

Clear glass baking dish (9 x 13-inch or larger recommended)

Warm water

Ice pack or a zip-top plastic bag full of ice cubes

M&M's

What to do:

1. Fill the baking dish with about 1 inch of warm water.
2. Place the ice pack at one end of the pan.
3. Place one of the M&M's in the water near the ice pack.
4. Watch as the color spreads. Does the color make a comet tail?

   (If the color doesn't make a comet tail, your dish might not be flat on the bottom. In this case, remove the ice pack, slide a thin kitchen towel under one edge of the dish, and try again. The candy color should flow downhill and form a comet tail.)

Color from dissolving M&M's forms a comet shape.

What's happening:

The ice pack cools the water around it. Since cold water is denser than warm water, the cold water sinks to the bottom of the pan. This pushes the bottom layer of water toward the other side of the pan. The moving water carries along the color from the dissolving M&M's, forming the comet shape. The white coating underneath the colored candy shell adds white streaks as it dissolves.

Comet tails in space form in a similar way. As a comet, or chunk of rock and ice, approaches the sun, the sun's radiation vaporizes some of the ice, creating vapor. The solar wind pushes the vapor away from the sun, forming the tail.

more fun

The cold water in your dish sinks, pushing the bottom layer of water toward the opposite edge of the dish. There the warm water rises and flows back toward the ice pack, forming a current. To see the water moving, add a drop of food coloring to your dish of water. You should see the food coloring on the bottom get pushed away from the ice, while the color on the surface moves toward the ice. If you watch long enough, you may even see some color rise to the surface and flow back toward the ice. (For the best view of this cycle, look through the side of the dish.)

CANDY COLOR TRAILS

Time: 5 minutes

Skill Level: Medium

What kind of candy floats away, leaving a trail of color?

What you need:

Clear glass baking dish (8-inch square or 9 x 13-inch)

Water

Cake Mate candy cake decorations

What to do:

1. Fill the dish about 1 inch deep with water.
2. Place one or more Cake Mate candies on the surface of the water. As the floating candy dissolves, color will sink to the bottom.
3. To make fun designs, give the candy a nudge or stir the water. As the candy floats away, it will leave a trail of color behind. (If the candy sinks too quickly, try another one. Cake Mate candies come in many different shapes, and some float better than others.)

What's happening:

Cake Mate candies are made from cake icing, which has been whipped and contains lots of air bubbles. This makes the candies less dense than water, so they float. But when they dissolve, the resulting sugar water is denser than water. It sinks, making the candy color trails.

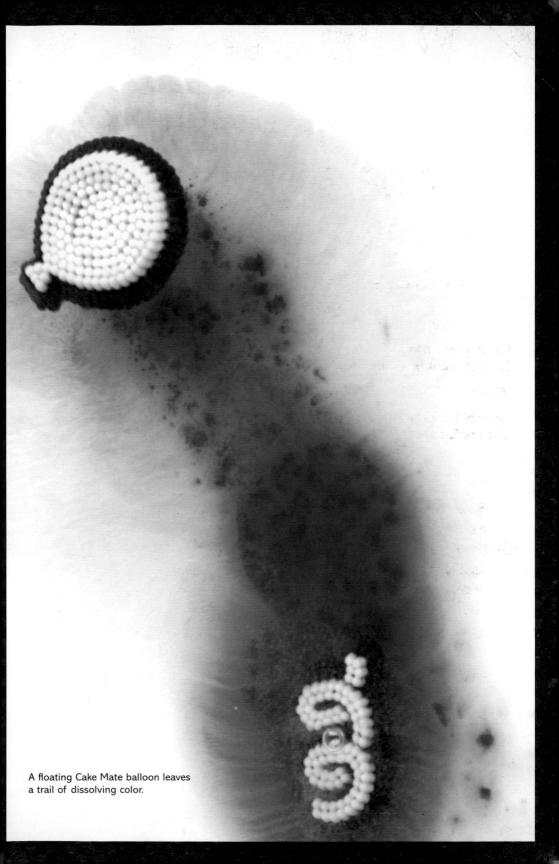

A floating Cake Mate balloon leaves
a trail of dissolving color.

FADE TO WHITE

Time: 1 week

Skill Level: Easy

Candy comes in beautiful colors. Can you change the color of your candy without touching it?

What you need:

Pink Necco Canada Mints or pink conversation hearts

Small glass jar (optional)

Zip-top plastic bag (optional)

What to do:

1. Find 2 pink candies that are exactly the same color.

2. Place one pink candy in a bright, sunny place, such as on a windowsill. If you put the candy outside, put it inside a glass jar to keep it safe from animals.

3. Place the other pink candy in a dark location, such as a cupboard. You may want to put it in a zip-top plastic bag to keep it safe.

4. After about 1 week, compare the two candies. Did the candy in the sunlight fade? (If not, put the candy back and wait longer.)

What's happening:

Candy is colored by dye. The dye contains colored molecules. If the dye molecules break apart, they lose their color.

When you put colored candy in the sun, the sunlight knocks electrons off the dye molecules and breaks them apart. As the colored molecules break down, the candy color fades.

Sunlight damages other kinds of molecules too, including the DNA molecules in your skin cells. This is why doctors say you should wear sunscreen for protection.

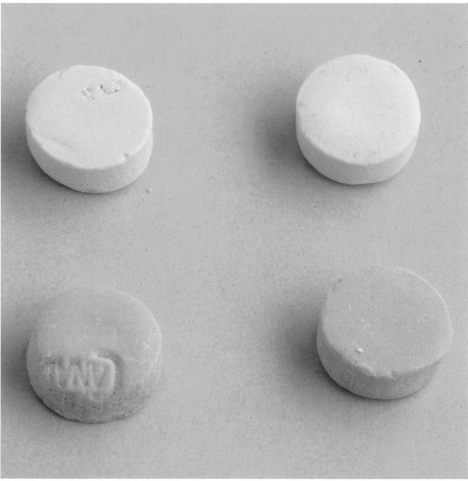

Pink mints (top) have faded after days in the sun.

SEPARATING CANDY COLORS

Time: 5 to 30 minutes

Skill Level: Medium

Some candy colors are a mix of several dyes. Can you unmix them?

What you need:

A glass filled with ½ inch of water

Plate, baking sheet, or piece of aluminum foil

Green or brown M&M's, green or purple Skittles, or other dyed candy

4-inch-long rectangle of coffee filter paper

Paper clips or clothespins (optional)

String, pencil, or small wire rack (optional)

What to do:

1. Sprinkle drops of water on the plate, baking sheet, or aluminum foil.

2. Put a candy on a water drop and let the color dissolve.

3. Dab or paint a splotch of the colored water onto the coffee filter paper, 1 inch from the bottom. (If you're testing several colors, label them with pencil.)

4. Stand the paper up in your glass, with the spot of color above the waterline. Use one of these methods:
   - Crease the paper vertically, then stand it up in the water.
   - Fold the top of the paper over the edge of the glass. (Note: If the wet paper touches the glass, the experiment may not work as well.)
   - Use paper clips or clothespins to clip the paper to a string, pencil, or rack over the glass.

5. Wait a few minutes.

6 When the water seeps up to the top of the paper, take the paper out. Did the colors spread?

What's happening:

As the water seeps up the paper, it dissolves the dyes and carries them along. The dyes that dissolve fastest are carried farthest. This separates the dyes.

For large groups:

If you try this experiment with friends or in a classroom, here's another way to make it work. Place several brown M&M's in a cup, add about 1 tablespoon of water, and use a paintbrush to dab the color from the dissolved M&M's onto the coffee filter paper. Fill a baking pan with ½ inch of water, and use clothespins to clip the chromatography papers onto a wire rack laid over the pan.

When you put filter paper in water to separate candy colors, you're doing **chromatography**.

M&M's color separation, or chromatography. Brown, on the right, has separated into a rainbow of colors.

Try this experiment with anything containing color, including juices, markers, or ballpoint pens.

CANDY RAINBOW IN A STRAW

Time: 5 to 10 minutes

Skill Level: Medium

Candy comes in all the colors of the rainbow. Can you make a rainbow with candy?

What you need:

5 small bowls

Warm water

M&M's or Skittles

Clear drinking straw

What to do:

1. Fill each of the bowls with 2 tablespoons of warm water.
2. Place one color of M&M's or Skittles in each bowl in these amounts:
   - 1 red
   - 2 orange
   - 3 yellow
   - 4 green
   - 5 blue (M&M's) or purple (Skittles)

3. Let candy shells dissolve. You do not need to dissolve the whole candy.

4. Dip your straw in the red bowl and suck up a small amount of red water (1 to 2 inches). Block the top of the straw with your tongue so you can move it to the next bowl. Repeat with orange, yellow, and so on.

5. Plug the bottom of your straw and hold it up. Can you see the rainbow?

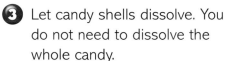

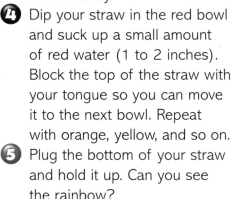

What's happening:

When sugar dissolves in water, it makes the water more dense. The more sugar is dissolved, the denser the water is. The densest water sinks, while less dense water floats on top. When you suck up the colors in order of density, the fluids float on each other, making a colored rainbow.

This should work for almost any kind of candy. If you dissolve more of one color than another color, the water with more dissolved candy will be more dense. What candy rainbows can you make?

Density rainbow in a straw.

Don't believe the dense water has to be on the bottom? Try sucking up blue, then red. If the densest fluid is on top, the colors will reverse position. The blue will sink to the bottom of the straw, and if you're lucky, the red will end up on top.

SKITTLES DENSITY RAINBOW

Time: 1 hour

Skill Level: Advanced

This experiment shows you how to layer different densities into a rainbow of color. (You may need help from a grown-up.)

What you need:

5 small microwave-safe cups

Skittles

Small clear drinking glass or small glass bowl

Liquid measuring cup (optional)

Wide metal spoon

Small bulb syringe or kitchen syringe (optional)

What to do:

1. Fill each cup with 2 tablespoons of water.
2. Dissolve the following amounts of Skittles, each color in a separate cup:
   - 2 red
   - 4 orange
   - 6 yellow
   - 8 green
   - 10 purple

For the experiment to work, the Skittles must dissolve completely. This can take up to an hour. To speed up the process, stir frequently or microwave each bowl for 30 seconds. **(Caution: hot!)**

3. When the candy is all dissolved, you may see an oily film or waxy debris floating on the water. If you like, scoop this off.
4. Pour the purple water into the clear glass or bowl.
5. **Optional:** Pour the green water into a liquid measuring cup. This will make it easier to pour out in step 7.
6. Hold the spoon upside down over the bowl so that the tip of the spoon touches the glass, with the tip ½ inch above the waterline.

7 Very slowly, pour the green over the back of the spoon so that the water drips down the tip of the spoon and down the side of the glass. The color should form a new layer on top of the purple. If it mixes with purple, you're pouring too fast.

8 Repeat with the other colors, and admire your rainbow.

What's happening:

Oil floats on water because the oil is less dense (lighter). Density also makes this rainbow work. The water with the most dissolved candy is the densest (the heaviest). Since the water with less candy is less dense, it floats on top of the denser water.

Unlike oil and water, your sugar water layers will eventually mix together, muddying the color. So admire your rainbow while it lasts!

Alternative method:

After step 4, use a small syringe to suck up the water from the green cup. Hold the tip of the syringe against the side of the purple bowl. Gently squeeze the syringe so that the green water runs down the bowl and floats on top of the purple water. Repeat with the other colors. This may be easier to control than the pouring method.

Skittles density rainbow.

more fun

You can also make rainbows with Nerds. Fill four cups each with ¼ cup warm water. Dissolve 1 teaspoon red Nerds, 2 teaspoons orange Nerds, 3 teaspoons yellow Nerds, and 4 teaspoons green Nerds (or whatever colors you like). Pour the rainbow the same way you poured it in the Skittles experiment.

Put a large marshmallow in a bowl of water. Push down on it. Do you feel the water pushing the marshmallow back up? When you let go, the marshmallow will pop to the surface. Now drop a Jolly Rancher in a bowl of water. It sinks straight to the bottom.

The marshmallow weighs a little bit more than the Jolly Rancher. So why does the Jolly Rancher sink and the marshmallow float?

A marshmallow is full of air bubbles, which make it bigger. Because the marshmallow is so big, it pushes away a lot of water when it starts to sink. All that water pushes back. The marshmallow floats.

The Jolly Rancher weighs almost as much as the marshmallow, but it's smaller. This means it is denser. It can't push aside as much water as the marshmallow, so the water doesn't push back as much. The Jolly Rancher sinks.

In this chapter, you'll sink and float all kinds of candy. Then learn how to float the unfloatable and sink the unsinkable!

chapter 3

SINK
AND FLOAT

HOW DENSE IS IT?

Time: 10 minutes

Skill Level: Advanced

Why does some candy sink, while some candy floats? To learn why a piece of candy sinks or floats, try this.

What you need:

Small cup or bowl, such as a ⅛-cup or ¼-cup measure, filled with water

Kitchen scale that measures grams

Pencil and paper

Tootsie Rolls, AirHeads, Laffy Taffy, taffy, or other soft candy you can squash

Large bowl of water

What to do:

1. Weigh the container of water and write down the weight.
2. Empty the container and dry it out.
3. Roll the candy between your palms to warm and soften it.
4. Squash the candy into the container until the container is full. Make sure there are no air pockets (empty spaces) between the candy and the container.
5. Weigh the container of candy and write down the weight.
6. Compare the weights. Does the candy weigh more than the water, or less? If it weighs more, it should sink in water.
7. Take the candy out of the container. (You may need to slide a table knife around the edge of the cup to unstick the candy.) Drop the candy into the large bowl of water. Did it sink? Were your calculations right?

Taffy weighs more than water. It is denser.

What's happening:

To find out whether a piece of candy will float, you need to know how much it weighs, and you need to know how much space it takes up (its volume). This tells you how dense the candy is. If ⅛ cup of candy weighs more than ⅛ cup of water, the candy is denser than the water. It will sink. If ⅛ cup of candy weighs less than ⅛ cup of water, it will float.

m o r e f u n

If you want to test the density of your candy, find a clear 2-cup liquid measuring cup. Weigh the empty cup. Then add water to reach the 1-cup measuring line. Weigh it, and subtract the weight of the empty cup to find the weight of the water.

One cup of Warheads (340 g) is denser than one cup of water.

Now add candy to the cup until the water reaches the 2-cup measuring line. If your candy floats, you will need to push it in until it is just below the waterline. Weigh it again, and subtract the previous weight. This will tell you how much your candy weighs. Does the candy weigh more or less than the water?

If you don't have enough candy to fill the cup, add enough candy to raise the water to the 1¼-cup line. Find the weight of the candy, and multiply that number by 4 to compare it with the weight of the water.

THE LIGHT CANDY BAR

Time: 1 to 5 minutes

Skill Level: Easy

Advertisements for 3 Musketeers bars say they're "light and fluffy." How light are they?

What you need:

3 Musketeers bar

Bowl of water big enough to hold the 3 Musketeers bar

What to do:

1. Drop 3 Musketeers bar into the water. Does it sink or float?
2. Break the candy bar in half. Do you see air bubbles inside the fluffy filling?
3. Put the candy bar halves back in the water. After a little while, they should sink. Can you see air bubbles escaping?

What's happening:

3 Musketeers bars are light because they're full of air bubbles. The air bubbles make the 3 Musketeers bar less dense than regular chocolate, so the candy bar floats.

Air bubbles inside a 3 Musketeers bar help it float.

Floating
3 Musketeers bar.

Other kinds of candy, such as marshmallows, Twix bars, or Whoppers, also have air trapped inside. Can you find more candy that floats?

FLOAT THE BOAT

Time: 5 minutes

Skill Level: Medium

If you drop a piece of taffy in water, it sinks like a rock. Can you make taffy float?

What you need:

Several pieces of taffy or other chewy candy, such as Laffy Taffy, Starburst, or Tootsie Rolls

Small bowl of water

What to do:

1. Drop one piece of taffy into the water. Does it sink?
2. Flatten another piece of taffy. Try pressing it between your hands, pushing on it with the back of a spoon, or using a rolling pin.
3. Mold the candy into the shape of a bowl or boat. Don't poke holes in it!
4. Gently place the candy in the water. Does it float?

What's happening:

A piece of candy floats when it pushes aside more water than it weighs. A square or ball of taffy doesn't push aside much water, so it sinks. But when you turn that taffy into a bowl, it can push aside enough water to float. You've made a taffy boat!

A large ship floats for this same reason. Even a ship made from metal, which is heavy, can push aside enough water to float.

These taffy boats float in water.

Having trouble floating your taffy? Try using foil, such as foil candy wrappers or aluminum foil, instead of candy. Crumple one piece of foil into a ball, and shape another piece into a bowl or boat. Which one floats? Which one sinks?

FLOAT THE UNFLOATABLE

Time: 5 minutes

Skill Level: Easy

Most candy sinks in water. Is there a way to float the unfloatable?

What you need:

2 cups

Regular soda (not sugar-free)

Water

2 pieces Laffy Taffy, or 2 mini Snickers, Nestlé Crunch, or Milky Way bars

What to do:

1. Fill one cup with soda and the other cup with water.
2. Drop one piece of candy in the soda and another piece in the water. Does the candy float in the soda?

What's happening:

Soda contains carbon dioxide gas. As bubbles form on the candy, they help lift it up, making the candy float in the soda. It's like a bubble life jacket!

Soda also contains sugar, making it denser than water. This is why some candy floats better in regular soda than in diet soda or club soda.

Laffy Taffy floating in cherry soda.

FLOAT THE REALLY UNFLOATABLE

Time: 5 minutes

Skill Level: Easy

Life Savers look like life preservers, the rings that help people float in the water. Can you float Life Savers candy?

What you need:

Molasses or corn syrup

Small bowl

1 mint Life Saver

What to do:

 Pour the molasses or corn syrup into the bowl.

② Place the Life Saver on the surface of the molasses. Does it float?

What's happening:

When you pour molasses or corn syrup, you see that it's thick and heavy. Molasses and corn syrup are both very dense. Since they're denser than Life Savers, the Life Saver floats.

Life Saver floating in molasses.

SINK THE UNSINKABLE

Time: 5 minutes

Skill Level: Easy

Twix bars float in water. Can you make them sink?

What you need:

2 small cups or bowls

Water

Cooking oil, such as vegetable oil*

2 mini Twix bars

What to do:

1 Half-fill one cup with water and the other cup with oil.

2 Place a Twix bar in your cup of water. Does it float? (Some Twix bars sink because they've been broken or squashed. If yours sinks, just try another one.)

3 Place the other Twix bar in your cup of oil. Does it sink?

What's happening:

Twix bars float in water because they're less dense than the water (think of all those trapped air bubbles). But oil weighs less than water, making it less dense. It's also less dense than the Twix bar. So the Twix bar sinks in oil.

°NOTE: Don't pour used oil down the drain. Once you're finished with the oil, seal it in a container, and put it in the garbage, or save it for more experiments.

Twix bars in water and in oil.

SQUASH THE UNSINKABLE

Time: 5 minutes

Skill Level: Easy

A 3 Musketeers bar floats as well as a boat. Can you sink a 3 Musketeers bar in water?

What you need:

3 Musketeers bar

Bowl of water big enough to hold the 3 Musketeers bar

What to do:

1. Drop the 3 Musketeers bar into the bowl of water. Does it float?
2. Take the candy bar out of the water.
3. Squash it into a ball.
4. Put it back in the water. Does it sink?

What's happening:

3 Musketeers bars float because the trapped air bubbles in the filling make the candy bar big and light. It pushes aside more water than it weighs.

When you squash it, you make the candy bar smaller. Since it can't push aside as much water, it sinks.

A squashed 3 Musketeers bar sinks in water.

HOW TO SINK A MARSHMALLOW

Time: 5 to 10 minutes

Skill Level: Medium

Marshmallows are filled with air, which makes them float. Can you sink them?

What you need:

Mini marshmallows

Large clear bowl of water

Cornstarch

Flat surface, such as a cutting board, tabletop, or counter

Spoon (optional)

What to do:

1. Drop a marshmallow into the water. Does it sink or float?
2. Sprinkle cornstarch over your flat surface.
3. Put the marshmallow on the cornstarch and squash it. Try rolling it, smashing it down, or smashing it between your hands. The cornstarch will keep it from getting too sticky.
4. Put it in water to see if it floats. (If it sticks to your hands, scrape it off with the spoon.)
5. The more you squash the marshmallow, the lower it will float in the water. If you squash it small enough, it will sink.
6. If your marshmallow didn't sink, grab another one and try again!

A squashed marshmallow sinks in water.

What's happening:

When you squash the marshmallow, you make it smaller and denser. The smaller it is, the less water it can push aside, and the lower it floats. If you squash the marshmallow so small that it's denser than water, it will sink.

Can't sink your marshmallow? Pour a cup of cooking oil, such as vegetable oil, into a bowl, and drop in your marshmallow. Since the oil is less dense than water, the marshmallow is more likely to sink.

If you're a champion at sinking mini marshmallows, try sinking large marshmallows. Can you beat the challenge?

MARSHMALLOW SUBMARINE

Time: 5 minutes

Skill Level: Easy

Marshmallows float in water. Can you make a marshmallow submarine that sinks?

What you need:

M&M's

Mini marshmallows

Large clear bowl of water

What to do:

1. Push one of the M&M's into the side of a marshmallow until it sticks. Add one more on the opposite side.
2. Drop your marshmallow submarine into the bowl of water. Does it sink?

What's happening:

To sink a marshmallow, you have to make it denser than water. This means you either need to make the marshmallow smaller or you need to add more weight to it.

When you add M&M's to the marshmallow, you make a submarine that's heavy enough to sink.

This marshmallow submarine sinks in water.

Can you add enough candy to a big marshmallow to make a sinking submarine? What about a chocolate-covered marshmallow, like a pumpkin or Santa?

FLOATING LETTERS

Time: 5 minutes

Skill Level: Easy

M&M's, Skittles, and Jelly Belly beans sink in water—mostly. To see what floats, try this.

What you need:

M&M's, Skittles, or Jelly Belly beans

Bowl of warm water

What to do:

1. Drop the candy into the bowl of water, logo side up.
2. Wait a few minutes. Do not stir the water.
3. After a few minutes, look for floating letters. (Some break up as they rise, but a few should survive intact.)

What's happening:

The white letters on M&M's, Skittles, and Jelly Belly beans are printed with an edible ink that doesn't dissolve in water. When the rest of the candy shell dissolves, the letters peel off and float.

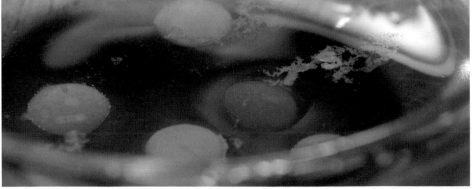

Floating Skittles.

HEARTS RISING

Time: 1 to 2 hours

Skill Level: Easy

Conversation hearts sink. Can you make them rise?

What you need:

Conversation hearts

Small clear bowl of water

What to do:

1. Put the conversation hearts into the bowl of water.
2. Wait about 2 hours. Do the hearts start to float?

What's happening:

The conversation hearts sink because they're denser than water. But as they sit in the water, air in the water forms bubbles on the hearts. The bubbles help the hearts float up to the surface.

more fun

How do you know that it's really the air in the water that makes the hearts float? Ask a grown-up to boil some water for you. Boiling the water will remove most of the air.

After the boiled water cools, pour some into a small bowl, pour water from the tap into a second cup, and put some hearts in each one. The hearts in the tap water will float sooner, because the tap water has more air in it.

HEARTS BOBBING

Time: 5 minutes

Skill Level: Easy

Hearts sink, and hearts float. Can you make them do both?

What you need:

Clear drinking glass

Club soda or clear soda

Conversation hearts or Necco wafers

What to do:

1. Fill the drinking glass with soda.
2. Put the candies in the glass. Do some of them float? Do they sink again? (If they don't sink by themselves, tap them with a spoon to knock off the bubbles.)

What's happening:

Club soda contains carbon dioxide gas. When the carbon dioxide forms bubbles on the candies, the candies start floating. It's as if they were wearing life jackets. But as the candies rise, the bubbles pop or get knocked off. Without the bubbles, the candies sink back to the bottom. Then bubbles start to form again, and the cycle starts over.

Brach's conversation hearts in 7UP.

Try this experiment with raisins.

How would you make a marshmallow bigger? By pulling on the corners? By stretching it out? Could you do it without using your fingers?

In this chapter, you'll learn all sorts of ways to make candy bigger—without touching it. Read on to find out how air, heat, or water can blow up your candy.

Caution: Some of these experiments involve heating candy in the microwave. Ask a grown-up to help you with these. Hot candy can be hotter than boiling water, so don't touch!

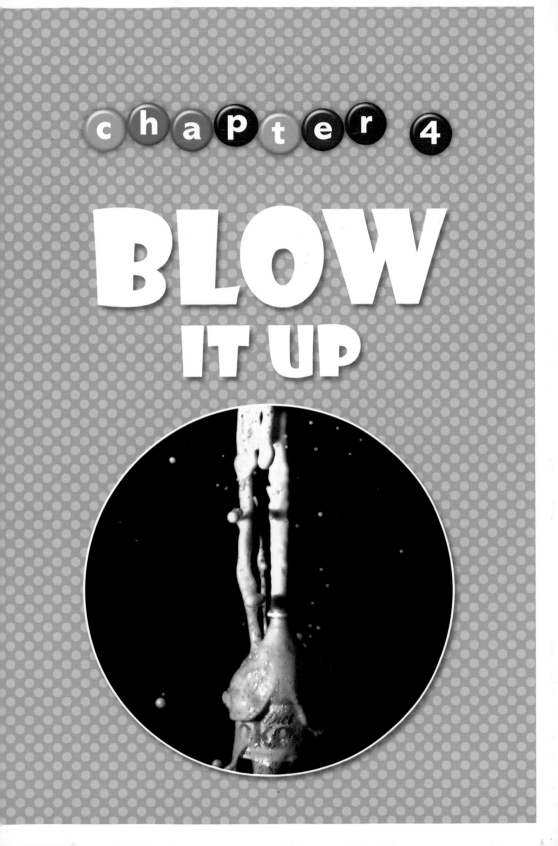

chapter 4

BLOW
IT UP

ENORMOUS EXPANDING MARSHMALLOW

Time: 5 minutes

Skill Level: Get a grown-up

Hot air puffs up a hot air balloon. You can try the same thing at home—in your microwave.

What you need:

Marshmallow or Peeps marshmallow candy

Microwave-safe plate

Microwave

What to do:

1. Put the marshmallow on the plate and microwave it to watch it expand (30 seconds to 1 minute).
2. When the microwave stops, open the door. As the marshmallow shrinks, listen for the hiss of air escaping from the marshmallow. Hold your hand over it—can you feel the hot air moving? **(Caution: hot! Don't touch the marshmallow!)**

What's happening:

Marshmallows are made of air bubbles trapped in a mix of water, sugar, and gelatin. When you microwave them, the water heats up, softening the sugar and warming the air. The hot air expands, pushing out the sides of the soft marshmallow like a balloon. But it can't last forever. As the marshmallow cools, the bubbles shrink and collapse as hot air escapes, leaving a puddle of marshmallow goo.

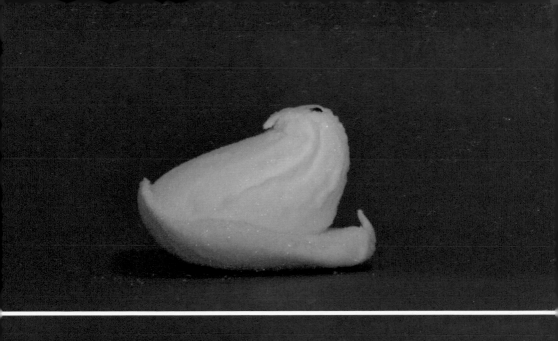

A Peeps chick becomes a giant chicken in the microwave.

Make a marshmallow pyramid with three on the bottom and one on top. Microwave the marshmallows. How tall does your pyramid get?

EXPANDING CANDY

Time: 5 minutes

Skill Level: Get a grown-up

You can microwave marshmallows and make them expand. Can you do this with any other candy?

What you need:

3 Musketeers bar (unwrapped)

Microwave-safe plate

Microwave

What to do:

1. Put the 3 Musketeers bar on the plate.
2. Microwave it until it expands and starts to bubble (30 seconds to 1 minute, depending on the size of the bar).

What's happening:

Like marshmallows, a 3 Musketeers bar contains air bubbles. When you microwave it, the air bubbles heat up and expand, pushing out the sides of the candy bar.

Microwaved 3 Musketeers bar.

more fun

What other candies contain air bubbles? Microwave them and see what happens.

MARSHMALLOW MOONSCAPE

Time: 5 minutes

Skill Level: Get a grown-up

Can you make a cratered moonscape in your microwave?

What you need:

Chocolate-covered marshmallow, such as a chocolate bunny, egg, pumpkin, or Santa

Microwave-safe plate

Microwave

What to do:

1. Put the chocolate-covered marshmallow on the plate.
2. Microwave it for 30 seconds to 1 minute. Do you see the marshmallow growing? Do you see how the chocolate creates craters in the marshmallow?

What's happening:

When you microwave a marshmallow, the air bubbles expand, pushing out the sides of the marshmallow (see the Enormous Expanding Marshmallow experiment on page 68). But the chocolate doesn't expand. Instead, it melts and breaks into pieces. These pieces weigh down the marshmallow, creating craters.

Marshmallow moonscape.

THE INCREDIBLE GROWING GUMMI WORM

Time: 2 hours to 2 days

Skill Level: Easy

Gummi candy grows bigger as it absorbs water. How big can your gummi get?

What you need:

Gummi candy containing gelatin, such as gummi worms, Life Savers Gummies, or gummi fruit snacks

Bowl of water

What to do:

1. Put the gummi candy in the bowl of water.
2. Check the candy after a few hours. Is it expanding?
3. Wait a couple of days. How big did your gummi candy grow? (Since different gummi candies are made using different recipes, some don't expand in water. If your candy didn't grow, try a different kind.)

What's happening:

"A dehydrated gummi worm is an unhappy gummi worm," says one scientist. That's because gummi worms absorb water. Lots of water.

Gummi candies are made with gelatin, a tangle of long protein molecules. (The tangled molecules don't break apart easily, which makes gummies stretchy.) When you put gelatin in water, the protein pulls the water into the tangle and the candy expands. Eventually, it absorbs so much water that the molecules spread apart and untangle, which makes the candy fall apart more easily.

As the gummi candy absorbs more and more water, it starts to resemble a different kind of gelatin dessert. Jell-O is also made of gelatin, sugar, and water. So when you expand your gummi candy, you're making something like Jell-O.

A two-day soak turns gummi worms into gummi snakes.

more fun

If you want to find out how much water your gummi worm absorbed, weigh it before and after the experiment. The added weight is the extra water. (If your gummi candy breaks, try lifting it with a slotted spoon or pouring the water and candy onto a plate.)

DANCING MARSHMALLOWS

Time: 15 minutes

Skill Level: Get a grown-up

Can you make marshmallows dance without touching them?

What you need:

Small bottle with a lid, such as an empty jam or peanut butter jar

A drill or a hammer and nail

Marshmallows

Rubber band

Bicycle pump

What to do:

1. Have a grown-up help you drill or hammer a hole through the lid of the jar. Try to make the hole the size of the bicycle pump nozzle.
2. Fill the jar with marshmallows.
3. Wrap the rubber band several times around the bicycle pump nozzle.
4. Insert the nozzle in the air hole in the lid of the jar. Slide the rubber band down to block air from escaping. Screw the lid onto the bottle.
5. Pump a few times. If too much air escapes from the bottle, try moving the rubber band to the underside of the lid to block air from that direction.
6. Pump air into the bottle and watch your marshmallows dance.

What's happening:

A marshmallow's size depends on air. Air bubbles inside the marshmallow push out, making it puffy. Air outside the marshmallow pushes in.

When you pump air into the bottle, air pushes against the marshmallows, causing them to shrink and move. When the air escapes from the bottle, the marshmallows expand back to their original size.

Pumping air into this bottle makes the marshmallows dance.

Try this with Peeps hearts. The hearts will look like they're actually beating.

VACUUM A MARSHMALLOW

Time: 5 minutes

Skill Level: Get a grown-up

Air bubbles inside a marshmallow push outward, but the air outside pushes back in. What happens if you remove some of the outside air?

What you need:

Marshmallows

FoodSaver vacuum sealer and container

What to do:

1. Place a marshmallow inside the FoodSaver container.
2. Seal the container.
3. With a grown-up's help, attach a hose to the container and to the vacuum sealer (see the FoodSaver instructions for more details).
4. Turn on the FoodSaver to vacuum air out of the container. Does the marshmallow expand? When you open the container to let air back in, does the marshmallow shrink? Does it look even smaller than when you started?

What's happening:

When you turn on the FoodSaver, you're vacuuming air out of the container. With less air pushing against the marshmallow, the air bubbles inside the marshmallow expand, making it grow.

After you unsealed the container, did your marshmallow look small and wrinkled? This may happen because air bubbles inside the marshmallow break open as the marshmallow expands, letting air leak out. With less air inside the marshmallow, it shrinks to a smaller size when the air pressure returns to normal.

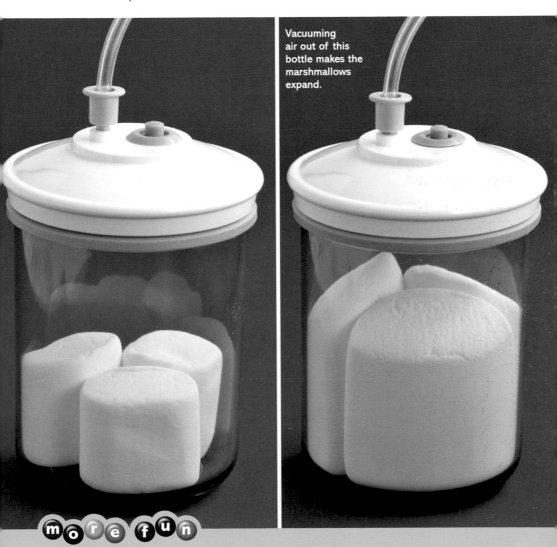

Vacuuming air out of this bottle makes the marshmallows expand.

more fun

Try filling the container half-full of marshmallows. When you turn on the vacuum, how much do the marshmallows expand?

MENTOS SODA FOUNTAIN

Time: 5 minutes

Skill Level: Medium

Did you know that candy can cause an eruption? To see how, try this. This experiment can get messy, so make the fountain outside, and wear old clothes.

What you need:

Toilet paper tube

Package of mint or fruit Mentos

2-liter bottle of Diet Coke

What to do:

1. Cut the toilet paper tube lengthwise, cut off a 1-inch-long strip, and then wrap the tube around the Mentos package. When you can easily slide the Mentos in and out, tape the sides together.
2. Open the Coke bottle and the Mentos package.
3. Fill the cardboard tube with Mentos. Block the bottom with the cardboard strip.
4. Hold the tube over the Coke bottle opening. When you're ready, remove the strip and let the Mentos fall into the Coke. Then get out of the way!

What's happening:

Soda pop is full of carbon dioxide gas. When you drop in Mentos, bubbles of carbon dioxide form on the surface of the candy. So many bubbles form so fast that they push the soda right out of the bottle.

Why use Mentos and Diet Coke? The rough surface of Mentos creates lots of places for bubbles to form. As they form, more carbon dioxide turns into gas and makes the bubbles bigger. More gas is released. Mentos also contain gum arabic, a surfactant, which decreases surface tension in the soda, so that bigger bubbles can grow. Diet Coke also contains surfactants.

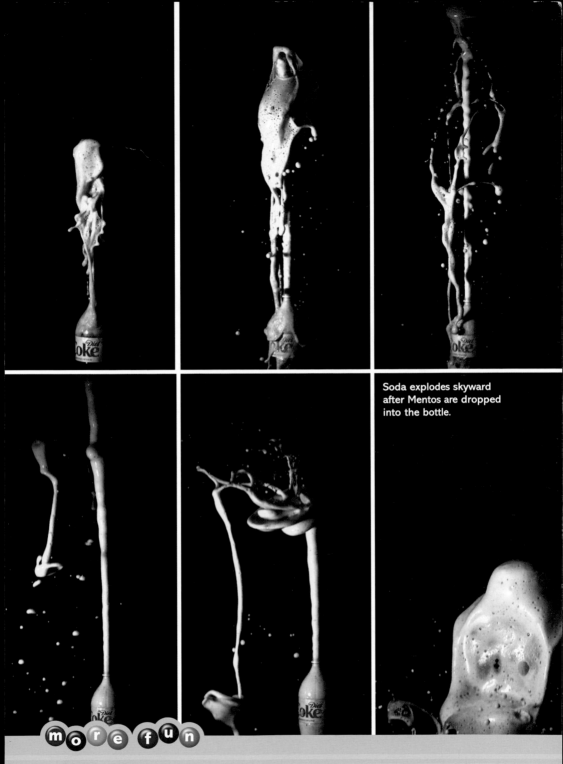

Soda explodes skyward after Mentos are dropped into the bottle.

more fun

Try dropping other kinds of candy in soda. Which kinds make the most bubbles? Do any work as well as Mentos?

Some candies break. Some candies stretch. And some just smoosh.

In this chapter, you'll discover different kinds of candies you can squash and what happens when you do. Learn how to shrink marshmallows without touching them, why you can stretch some kinds of candy into long snakes, and what kind of candy makes sparks when you smash it. Squash away!

chapter 5

SQUASH IT

MINI MARSHMALLOW SQUASH

Time: 5 minutes

Skill Level: Medium

Can you squash marshmallows without touching them?

What you need:

Baby soda bottle test tube (available at amazon.com) or a small clean plastic soda or water bottle

Mini marshmallows

Fizz-Keeper pump (available at amazon.com)

Rubber band

What to do:

1. Fill the test tube or bottle with mini marshmallows.
2. Screw the Fizz-Keeper onto the top.
3. If using a bottle, wrap the rubber band around the bottle and slide it to be level with the top of the marshmallows. This will mark the marshmallows' normal size.
4. Push the Fizz-Keeper handle to pump air into the bottle. As you pump, you'll see the marshmallows shrink.
5. Unscrew the Fizz-Keeper and watch the marshmallows pop back to their original size.

What's happening:

A marshmallow is shaped by air. Air bubbles inside the marshmallow push out, making it puffy. Air outside the marshmallow pushes in. The push of the air is called "air pressure."

When you pump the bottle, you're adding air to the bottle. This increases the air pressure. The air pushes harder against the marshmallows, shrinking the air bubbles inside.

When you unscrew the lid, the air inside the marshmallows pushes out, expanding them back to their original size.

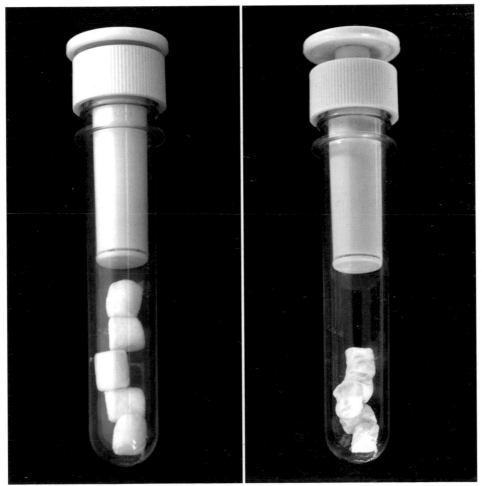

Marshmallows shrink when air is pumped into this test tube.

MARSHMALLOW AQUA-SQUASH

Time: 15 minutes

Skill Level: Medium

Can you squash a marshmallow with water?

What you need:

1 large marshmallow or several small marshmallows

Waxed paper or parchment paper

Small empty soda bottle with the cap

Water

What to do:

 Wrap the large marshmallow tightly in a piece of waxed paper or parchment paper. Slide the paper into the bottle, holding tight to the corner. Shake the marshmallow into the bottle and pull the paper out. Alternatively, put several small marshmallows into the bottle.

 Fill the bottle with water to the very top and screw on the cap. (Try not to leave any air bubbles.)

Squeeze the bottle. Do you see the marshmallow shrink?

What's happening:

When you squeeze the bottle, you're applying pressure. The pressure squeezes the air bubbles in the marshmallow, making the marshmallow smaller. When you release the bottle, the air bubbles push the marshmallow back to its normal size.

Squeezing this bottle of water shrinks the marshmallows inside.

more fun

If you leave the marshmallow in the bottle for several days, it will dissolve, and you'll see bubbles. Where do you think they came from?

STRETCHY SNAKE

Time: 5 to 10 minutes

Skill Level: Easy

You can roll play dough into long, stretchy snakes. Can you do it with candy?

What you need:

Soft chewy candy, such as taffy, Laffy Taffy, or Tootsie Rolls

Cutting board or other surface for rolling

Butter (optional)

What to do:

1. If the taffy is hard, roll it between your palms to soften it.
2. Put the taffy on the cutting board, press down, and start to roll. (You may want to butter your hands to keep the candy from sticking.) As you roll, move your hands apart to stretch the candy out. How long can you make your stretchy snake?

What's happening:

Taffy contains a lot of sugar and a little bit of water. Sugar and water stick together. The molecules are attracted to each other, which makes them hard to pull apart. But water can also act as a lubricant between the sugar molecules. This means it helps the molecules slide apart more easily. So, if the candy has the right mix of sugar and water, and if the sugar molecules are not locked into crystals, the candy can stretch.

The sugar and water in this taffy help it stretch.

BUTTERSCOTCH BREAK

Time: 5 minutes

Skill Level: Get a grown-up

Can you break your candy like a rock?

What you need:

Werther's butterscotch candy, striped starlight mints, Jolly Ranchers, or other hard, glassy candy

A way to smash candy, such as a sidewalk and a rock or hammer, or a cutting board and a marble rolling pin

What to do:

1 Smash the butterscotch candy so that it cracks into two or more pieces. Ways to smash your candy (ask a grown-up for help):

- Set it down on a sidewalk and hit it with a rock.
- Put it on pavement and tap it gently with a hammer.
- Put it on a cutting board and tap it with a marble rolling pin.

2 Look for curved surfaces along the break lines. These scooped-out shapes might look like the surfaces of seashells.

What's happening:

In butterscotch candy, the sugar molecules haven't formed crystals. Instead, they're all jumbled together. This kind of substance is called a "glass." Window glass is also made from a jumble of molecules.

When you break certain kinds of crystals, the breaks follow the lines of the crystal structure. But when you break a glass, the force can go in any direction. This can cause the glass to break with curved edges. Sometimes shock waves traveling through the glass even leave small ripples on the broken surface. You might see these ripples in your broken candy.

Glassy rocks also break with curved edges. One of these rocks is obsidian, a glassy rock formed when hot lava cools quickly. Geologists (scientists who study rocks) look at broken edges when they are trying to identify different kinds of rocks.

The curving breaks in glassy candy are called **conchoidal fractures**.

Curved breaks in butterscotch candy and obsidian rock.

LIFE SAVERS LIGHTS

Time: 5 minutes

Skill Level: Easy or Medium

Can you make Life Savers spark in the dark?

What you need:

Dark room with a mirror

Wintergreen Life Savers

Mortar and pestle (optional)

Baking sheet (optional)

What to do:

Chewing method (easy):

1. Stand in the dark room facing the mirror. (If you don't have a mirror, get a partner so you can watch each other.)
2. Chew a Life Saver with your mouth open.
3. Look for flashes of light.

Mortar and pestle method (medium):

1. Put the mortar and pestle on the baking sheet.
2. Take the baking sheet and Life Savers into the dark room. (You can leave the light on.) Lay the baking sheet on the floor, on a counter, or on your lap. The baking sheet will help catch crumbs.
3. Put the Life Savers in the mortar.
4. Turn off the light.
5. Smash the Life Savers with the mortar and pestle, and look for flashes of light. (Save the smashed candy for Candy Crystals on page 128.)

What's happening:

When you crunch the candy, electrons in the sugar crystals are separated from the molecules. When the electrons recombine with the molecules, they emit light.

Table sugar also emits light when the crystals are broken, but much of that light is ultraviolet, which we can't see. Wintergreen oil absorbs that light and re-emits it in a visible frequency. That's why wintergreen Life Savers give off so much more light than sugar cubes.

This experiment works because wintergreen Life Savers contain sugar crystals and wintergreen oil. See if you can make lights with any other kinds of wintergreen candy, such as Altoids. (Sugar-free mints won't work.)

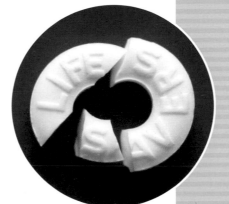

Smashing wintergreen Life Savers makes sparks in the dark.

Why does one Life Saver melt into a bubbling puddle, while another hot Life Saver stays solid? Why does a Smartie melt faster than an Altoid? What kind of candy makes water cold?

In this chapter, you'll melt Life Savers and shatter taffy. You'll have races between different kinds of candy to see what melts faster. You'll turn Skittles into gaping clamshells. You'll learn how hot and cold change everything!

CAUTION: IT'S HOT!

Think boiling water is hot? Melted candy can be much hotter. To be safe, always have a grown-up help you heat candy in the microwave or the oven. Watch the candy as it melts. If it starts turning brown or black, or starts to smoke, turn off the heat. Use hot pads to pick up hot plates or dishes. Never touch hot candy with your bare fingers (if you want to see how soft it is, poke it with a fork). Never melt a jawbreaker, because it can explode and cause terrible burns.

chapter 6

HOT
AND COLD

MICROWAVE MELTING RACES

Time: 5 minutes

Skill Level: Get a grown-up

Some candies turn soft and fluid in the microwave, but which ones?

What you need:

Starburst, Tootsie Rolls, Laffy Taffy, taffy, or other soft candy

Microwave-safe plate

Block of wood

Microwave

What to do:

1. Place the candies in a straight line on one side of your plate. This will be the "starting line."

2. Set the plate in the microwave with the "start" side on the block of wood so that the plate slants. This will be your race ramp.

3. Microwave for 30 seconds to 1 minute, and watch your heated candy flow down the plate. Which kind wins?

What's happening:

Most chewy candy turns soft and fluid when it's heated. How fast this happens depends on many things, including what shape it is, what kind of sugar it's made from, and how much water it contains. Since softer candy contains more water (it makes the candy soft and chewy), it becomes fluid at a lower temperature than hard candy.

Are these really melting races? Not quite. Melting happens when you heat up a solid (like an ice cube) to change it into a liquid (water). Chewy candy is already a kind of liquid, even if it's pretty hard. When you heat it up, you're just making the candy more fluid.

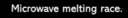

Microwave melting race.

LIFE SAVERS MELTING RACE

Time: 5 to 10 minutes

Skill Level: Get a grown-up

What's the difference between a mint Life Saver and a cherry Life Saver? They're both hard. They're both sweet. How different could they be? Actually, a mint Life Saver and a fruit-flavored Life Saver are very different. To see one of these differences, just turn on the oven.

What you need:

Oven

1 fruit-flavored Life Saver

1 white mint Life Saver

Aluminum foil–lined baking sheet

What to do:

1. Preheat the oven to 300°F.
2. Place the two Life Savers on the baking sheet.
3. Heat the Life Savers in the oven for 5 to 10 minutes. What happens? **(Caution: hot! Don't touch the hot candy.)**

What's happening:

Compare a Legos structure with a basket full of Legos pieces. If you shake them both, which Legos come apart?

Like Legos, the molecules in the mint Life Saver are locked together, forming crystals. You see the same kind of white crystals when you look in your sugar bowl.

The fruit-flavored Life Saver is made from sugar mixed with corn syrup, which contains many different kinds of molecules. These molecules don't bond together, so they don't form crystals. Instead, they make a jumble, like the Legos in the basket.

When you heat the Life Savers, the molecules vibrate. Since the molecules in the mint Life Saver are locked into crystals, they hold together. But in the fruit-flavored Life Saver, the unconnected molecules slide apart. The candy becomes softer and more liquid, spreading out into a puddle.

Life Savers melting race: mint vs. cherry.

ALTOIDS VS. SMARTIES MELTING RACE

Time: 5 to 10 minutes

Skill Level: Get a grown-up

They're both round. They're both made of sugar. So which one melts first, Smarties or Altoids?

What you need:

Oven

Altoids

Smarties

Aluminum foil–lined baking sheet

What to do:

1. Preheat the oven to 250°F.
2. Place one Altoid and one Smartie on the baking sheet.
3. Put the baking sheet in the oven.
4. After 5 to 10 minutes, check your candy. Which one melted?

What's happening:

Altoids and Smarties are made of different kinds of sugar. Altoids are made from sucrose (table sugar). Smarties are made from a different kind of sugar, dextrose (also called "glucose"). Dextrose melts at a lower temperature than sucrose, so the Smartie melts first.

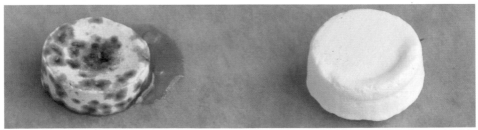

Melting race: Smarties vs. Altoids.

CLAMSHELL SKITTLES

Time: 2 to 5 minutes

Skill Level: Get a grown-up

Can you crack Skittles open like clamshells?

What you need:

Skittles

Microwave-safe plate

Microwave

Alternative:
Aluminum foil–lined baking sheet

Oven

What to do:

1 Place the Skittles on the plate and microwave them for 1 to 2 minutes. (Alternatively, place the Skittles on the baking sheet and melt them in the oven at 350°F for about 5 minutes.)

2 Do the Skittles crack open like clams?

What's happening:

Since the insides of the Skittles are soft, they contain more water than the outside sugar shells. This means the insides will soften faster when they get hot, spilling out the sides.

Do some of the Skittles open up like clamshells? Perhaps the hot candy on the inside is creating steam, which pushes up the tops of the Skittles.

Melted Skittles clamshells.

CRAZY CANES

Time: 10 to 30 minutes

Skill Level: Get a grown-up

Snap! That's what happens to your candy cane if you try to bend it. Is there a way to bend candy canes without breaking them?

What you need:

Oven

Aluminum foil

Baking sheet

Candy cane or straight candy stick

What to do:

1. Preheat the oven to 250°F.
2. Tear off a square of aluminum foil. Fold it in half, then fold again and again to make a rectangular strip about 3 inches wide (wider than the candy cane). Bend this strip into a fun shape, like a zigzag, an S-curve, or a bowl.
3. Place the foil shape on the baking sheet and put the candy cane on the foil shape. Heat in the oven for 5 to 20 minutes. (The melting time will depend on the size of the candy cane.) Check frequently until the candy cane has softened and curved into the shape of the mold.

What's happening:

When you're melting an ice cube, you can see it turn to water. An ice cube is a solid, made from molecules locked together as crystals. When it melts, the molecules break apart. The solid becomes a liquid.

The molecules in a candy cane don't make crystals. Instead, the candy cane contains lots of kinds of molecules jumbled together, like the fruit Life Saver in the Life Savers Melting Race experiment on page 96. When it gets warm, it doesn't turn liquid right away. Instead, it gets softer and softer as the molecules shift around. That's why you can turn a warm candy cane into a crazy cane.

In fact, your candy cane has already been heated and bent. A candy cane is made from a straight candy stick that's bent into a cane shape while it's still warm.

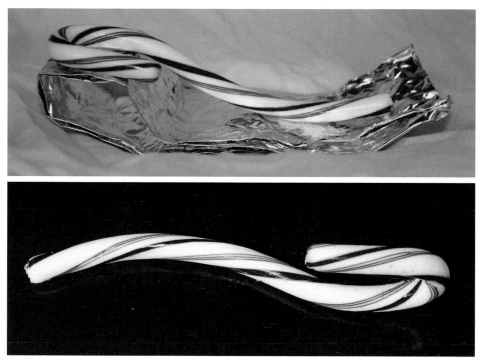

Melted candy canes turn into crazy canes.

RUBBER BANDY CANES

Time: 10 to 15 minutes

Skill Level: Get a grown-up

Here's how you can stretch one brand of candy canes like rubber bands.

What you need:

Oven

Bobs brand candy cane

Aluminum foil–lined baking sheet

2 pairs of tongs

What to do:

1. Preheat the oven to 250°F.
2. Put the candy cane on the baking sheet and place it in the oven.
3. Wait about 5 minutes, until the candy cane is warm but not yet melting. Remove the pan from the oven.
4. Using the 2 pairs of tongs, pick up the candy cane and break it apart. Does the middle stretch?

What's happening:

In this type of candy cane, the middle section apparently melts at a lower temperature than the outside. That's why the outside breaks, but the middle stretches.

These broken candy canes stretch like rubber bands.

SHATTER TAFFY

Time: A few hours

Skill Level: Easy

Taffy bends and stretches. Can you shatter it?

What you need:

AirHeads taffies
(do not unwrap them)

Freezer

What to do:

1. Place the AirHeads in the freezer for several hours.
2. Unwrap the AirHeads and bend them. Did they crack?

What's happening:

Warm molecules move around. When you bend the taffy, the molecules shift, still holding together. This means you can stretch and bend your taffy.

When you freeze the taffy, the molecules don't move as much. Instead of shifting when you bend the taffy, they are more likely to simply come apart. Crack! Your taffy shatters.

Warm AirHeads stretch, but frozen AirHeads break.

CANDY WATER COOLER

Time: 5 to 10 minutes

Skill Level: Easy

Can you make water cold without adding ice cubes?

What you need:

3 small bowls

Room-temperature water

6 or more Pixy Stix

Kitchen thermometer (optional)

What to do:

1. Fill 2 of the bowls with ¼ cup of water each.
2. Break open the Pixy Stix and pour the candy powder into the third, empty bowl.
3. Pour the Pixy Stix powder into one bowl of water and stir. Leave the other bowl alone. It will be your "control" (the one that doesn't change).
4. Touch the water in both bowls. Does the Pixy Stix water feel colder? Compare the temperatures with the kitchen thermometer.

What's happening:

The sugar powder in the Pixy Stix is made from sugar molecules locked together into crystals. It takes energy to break up those crystals and separate the molecules. This energy comes from the heat in the water. So as the sugar dissolves, absorbing energy from the water, the water gets colder.

Many kinds of sugar absorb energy when they dissolve, making water cool. Even table sugar (sucrose) does this, although it's hard to detect that change without a thermometer. Dextrose, the kind of sugar in Pixy Stix, absorbs a lot of energy when it dissolves, making the water much cooler. That's why you can feel the temperature change with your bare fingers.

Pixy Stix candy makes water colder.

Try this experiment with candy made from dextrose (glucose), mannitol, erythritol, sorbitol, or xylitol. First, crush the candy into small pieces to help it dissolve quickly. Then add it to the water.

An **endothermic reaction** absorbs heat from its surroundings.

CANDY WATER HEATER

Time: 15 minutes

Skill Level: Get a grown-up

Can you warm up water without using the microwave?

What you need:

3 small bowls

Room-temperature water

6 Jolly Ranchers

2 zip-top plastic bags

Rolling pin or hammer

Kitchen thermometer

What to do:

1. Fill two of the bowls with ¼ cup of water each.
2. Put the Jolly Ranchers in a zip-top bag, zip it closed, then put that bag inside the second zip-top bag. (This will help keep fragments from escaping when you smash the candy.)
3. Smash the candy into very small pieces. If you're indoors, put the bag on a cutting board and smash the candy with a rolling pin. If you're outdoors, put the bag on the pavement and smash the candy with a rock or a hammer.
4. Open the bag and pour the candy into one bowl of water.
5. Test the temperature in each bowl of water with the thermometer. Is the Jolly Rancher water a little bit warmer?

An **exothermic reaction** releases heat into its surroundings.

What's happening:

When sugar crystals dissolve, the molecules must absorb energy to break apart. This makes the water cold (see the Candy Water Cooler experiment on page 104).

But Jolly Ranchers aren't made from sugar crystals. They're made from sugar and corn syrup, which has many different kinds of molecules. These molecules can't lock together to make crystals (that would be like trying to combine Legos with Tinkertoys). Instead, the molecules are all jumbled together. So the candy doesn't need to absorb energy when it dissolves. Instead, it releases energy, making the water a little bit warmer.

Shattered Jolly Ranchers warm up water.

COOL MINT?

Time: 5 minutes

Skill Level: Get a grown-up

Mint candy tastes "cool" on your tongue. Does it really cool things down?

What you need:

Room-temperature water

4 small bowls

Digital thermometer (must measure increments of 0.1°F)

5 or more starlight mints

12 or more Eclipse mints or other mints made from dextrose, sorbitol, maltitol, erythritol, or xylitol

4 zip-top plastic bags

Cutting board and rolling pin

Peppermint extract (optional)

What to do:

1 Pour ¼ cup water into each bowl. With your thermometer, check that the temperature is the same in each bowl. (If it isn't, pour all the water together and measure it out again.)

2 Place the starlight mints in a zip-top plastic bag, and put that bag inside a second zip-top bag. Put the Eclipse mints in another set of zip bags.

3 Smash the bagged candy to powder. If indoors, put the bags on a cutting board and smash with a rolling pin or something else hard. If outdoors, put the bags on the pavement and smash with a rock or a hammer.

4 Pour the starlight mints into one bowl of water. Stir and measure the temperature.

5 Pour the Eclipse mints into another bowl of water. Stir and measure the temperature.

6 If testing peppermint extract, pour ¼ teaspoon into a third bowl of water. Stir and measure the temperature.

7 Test the temperature in each bowl again, since the temperatures might change as more candy dissolves. Compare these temperatures with the water in your fourth bowl (your control sample). Did any of your experiments get warmer? Did any get cooler? (You will probably not be able to feel the temperature difference with your fingers.)

What's happening:

You might think that peppermint candy makes your mouth cooler. But some of it actually makes your mouth a little bit warmer! What's going on?

In these experiments, it's not the peppermint changing the water temperature. Instead, it's what the peppermint is mixed with. The starlight mints contain corn syrup, which releases a little heat when it dissolves in water. The peppermint extract contains alcohol, which also releases a little heat when it mixes with water.

The Eclipse mints, on the other hand, contain maltitol and sorbitol. These two sweeteners absorb heat when they dissolve, so they do make the water cooler. Many other sweeteners also absorb heat when they dissolve (see the Candy Water Cooler experiment on page 104). Candy makers sometimes use these sweeteners in mints because they make your mouth feel colder and "mintier."

So why does peppermint taste "cool?" Scientists think that the menthol in peppermint might trigger the same receptors on your skin that tell your nerves when it's cold. In other words, the mint feels cold even if it isn't.

Which mint actually cools water?

Broken candy dissolves faster than whole candy. Cotton candy dissolves into slime. Chocolate doesn't dissolve in water, and gum doesn't dissolve at all. Or does it?

In this chapter, you'll learn how to make candy dissolve faster, what kind of candy dissolves into slime, how to dissolve everything but the candy shell, and what part of a Tootsie Roll you can unroll yourself. Start dissolving!

chapter 7

DISSOLVE THIS!

RACE TO DISSOLVE (BIG VS. SMALL)

Time: 5 to 30 minutes

Skill Level: Get a grown-up

Does candy dissolve faster if you break it up?

What you need:

2 bowls

Warm water

2 identical pieces of colored candy, such as Jolly Ranchers, or small candy, such as conversation hearts, Pez, or Tic Tacs

What to do:

1. Fill each bowl with about 1 cup of warm water.
2. Break or crush one candy into small pieces.
3. Put the unbroken candy into one bowl of water. Put the pieces of the broken candy into the other bowl of water.
4. Watch to see which dissolves faster. If you're using colored candy, watch the bottom of the bowl. The broken pieces should dissolve faster, coloring the bottom of the bowl.
5. If you see candy pieces floating hours later, poke or stir them to see if they've dissolved. Sometimes what looks like a floating piece of candy is just a collection of leftover bubbles.

What's happening:

Candy dissolves in water. But it doesn't dissolve all at once. The outer edge (or surface) dissolves first, because that's the part that touches the water.

When you put in one big piece of candy, only the outer surface touches the water. The candy dissolves slowly.

When you break the candy into pieces, you create more surfaces. More of the candy touches the water. This helps the candy to dissolve more quickly.

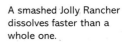

A smashed Jolly Rancher dissolves faster than a whole one.

Try this experiment with other kinds of candy. What else dissolves faster after you smash it?

RACE TO DISSOLVE (HOT VS. COLD)

Time: 5 to 30 minutes

Skill Level: Easy

Does candy dissolve faster in hot or cold water?

What you need:

2 small bowls or cups

Warm and cold water

Ice cubes (optional)

2 identical pieces of candy, such as Skittles, Jolly Ranchers, Starbursts, Tootsie Rolls, lollipops, small chocolates, or chocolate bars

What to do:

1. Fill one bowl with warm water and one bowl with cold water. For better results, add ice cubes to the cold water.
2. Put one candy in the warm bowl and one in the cold bowl.
3. Watch to see which dissolves faster.

Skittles in warm water (left) dissolve faster than Skittles in ice water (below).

What's happening:

Candy dissolves when the molecules in the candy, such as sugar, mix together with the water molecules. Because molecules move faster when the temperature is hot, the candy in hot water dissolves much faster. The candy in ice water might take all night to dissolve.

Chocolate, on the other hand, won't ever dissolve in cold water. That's because chocolate is made from cocoa butter, which is a kind of oil. Oil doesn't dissolve in water, and so neither does chocolate. But in hot water, the cocoa butter melts and mixes with the water.

DEFYING GRAVITY WITH COTTON CANDY SLIME

Time: 1 minute

Skill Level: Easy

Water always flows downhill—or does it? To find out, you just need the right kind of candy.

What you need:

Cotton candy

Bowl of water

What to do:

1. Dip a piece of cotton candy fluff in the water.
2. Watch the water zoom up the cotton candy strands before they dissolve into slime! (If the water doesn't zoom upward, squash the cotton candy fluff and try again.)

What's happening:

In a glass of water, the water near the edges rises to touch the glass. That's because the water is attracted to the glass.

Water is also attracted to the fibers in a paper towel. When you dip a paper towel in water, the water seeps up. Because the paper towel's fibers are so close together, the water's attraction to the fibers becomes stronger than the pull of gravity. (This is also what makes the Separating Candy Colors experiment on page 36 work.)

The strands of spun sugar in cotton candy attract water just like the fibers in a paper towel. The closer together the strands are, the faster the water seeps up (that's why squashing the cotton candy makes the experiment work better). As the water climbs, it dissolves the sugar, leaving candy water slime.

Cotton candy soaks up water.

more fun

Sprinkle a few drops of water onto your cotton candy. The water drops dissolve the cotton candy, eating their way through the candy fluff like caterpillars.

HOLLOW CANDY SHELLS

Time: 30 minutes to several hours

Skill Level: Easy

Can you turn a chocolate candy into a hollow shell?

What you need:

Chocolate candy with sugary filling, such as Rolo, Caramello bars, 3 Musketeers bars, Junior Mints, Whoppers, Robin Eggs, or Cadbury Creme Eggs

Bowl of water

What's happening:

Chocolate doesn't dissolve in water. But sugar does. So candy fillings that are made mostly of sugar, like mint filling or caramel, dissolve in water. This leaves behind a hollow chocolate shell.

What to do:

1. Break or cut the chocolate candy in half, so that the filling is exposed.
2. Put the candy into the bowl of water.
3. Leave the candy there for up to several hours. Has the filling disappeared?

Dissolving the candy filling makes hollow chocolate shells.

DISSOLVING GUM

Time: 5 to 10 minutes

Skill Level: Medium

Chewing gum doesn't dissolve, does it? To find out, try this.

What you need:

Piece of gum (do not unwrap it)

Kitchen scale

Bowl of water (optional)

What to do:

1. Weigh the piece of gum before unwrapping it. Then unwrap it but save the wrapper.
2. Chew the gum for several minutes. Alternatively, put the gum in a bowl of water. Smash and stretch it with your fingers as if you were "chewing" it.
3. Weigh the piece of gum on the wrapper. Does it weigh less?

What's happening:

Chewing gum is made from gum base and sugar (or some other sweetener). Gum base, the stretchy stuff, doesn't dissolve in water. (Gum base is actually a kind of rubber.) But the sugar does dissolve. So as you chew, the sugar in your chewing gum dissolves into your saliva, or into the bowl of water. That's why gum weighs less after you chew it.

Does this gum really dissolve?

DISSOLVING CHOCOLATE

Time: 10 minutes

Skill Level: Medium

Chocolate doesn't dissolve in cold water. Can you dissolve it in anything else?

What you need:

Cold water

2 small bowls

2 small pieces of chocolate

Cooking oil, such as vegetable oil*

Paper towel (optional)

What to do:

1. Pour cold water into one bowl. Put a few tablespoons of oil in the other bowl (enough to cover the chocolate).
2. Put a small piece of chocolate in each bowl and wait about 10 minutes.
3. Pick up the chocolate in the water. Does it feel any different?
4. Pick up the chocolate in the oil. Does it rub off onto your fingers? You can also rub it against a paper towel to see the dissolved chocolate.

What's happening:

If you pour water and oil together, eventually the oil will float on top of the water. That's because oil and water don't mix. Oil doesn't dissolve in water, and water doesn't dissolve in oil. Some things that dissolve in water (like salt) will not dissolve in oil, and vice versa.

Chocolate is made from cocoa butter. Cocoa butter is a type of fat, or oil, which means that it doesn't dissolve in water. But since it's a type of oil, it does dissolve in cooking oil.

Chocolate dissolving in oil.

*NOTE: Don't pour used oil down the drain. Once you're finished with the oil, seal it in a container, and put it in the garbage; or save it for more experiments.

TOOTSIE UNROLLING

Time: Several hours

Skill Level: Easy

Tootsie Rolls aren't the only kind of roll in a Tootsie Pop. To find out what else there is, try this.

What you need:

Tootsie Pop stick, or other lollipop stick that is not plastic

Shallow dish or cup of water

What to do:

1 Put the lollipop stick in the water.

2 Wait for several hours, or until the lollipop stick is completely soaked.

3 Pull out the stick. Can you unroll it?

What's happening:

Many lollipop sticks are made of paper that's been rolled into tight rolls. This makes the paper stronger. When the sticks get wet, they unroll.

A wet Tootsie Pop stick unrolls.

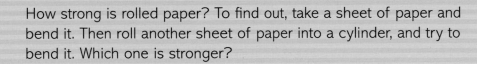

How strong is rolled paper? To find out, take a sheet of paper and bend it. Then roll another sheet of paper into a cylinder, and try to bend it. Which one is stronger?

What do sucrose (table sugar), table salt, ice cubes, and diamonds have in common? They're all made of crystals. Their molecules are locked together in regular shapes, like the way Legos lock together.

Some kinds of candy also contain crystals. Rock candy, which looks like clear colored blocks stuck together around a stick, is made of sugar crystals and food coloring. (The large sugar crystals make the blocks.) The sugar crystals in wintergreen Life Savers create flashes of light when you crush them. Chocolate bloom happens when the cocoa butter changes from one crystal form to another.

Some kinds of candy don't contain crystals, like glassy Jolly Ranchers or chewy taffy. These candies are made with corn syrup. The corn syrup molecules come in different shapes that don't lock together. This prevents crystals from forming. Oil is also added to candy to prevent crystals.

In this chapter, you'll learn how to make crystals with different kinds of candy, and what kind of candy will never crystallize.

To dissolve the candy for these experiments, you'll need to heat it in water. Ask a grown-up to help you because these mixtures will be very hot.

chapter 8

CRYSTALS

ROCK CANDY CRYSTALS

Time: About 1 week

Skill Level: Get a grown-up

Rock candy is made from sugar crystals. Here's how you can make sugar crystals at home.

What you need:

Table sugar

Water

Small microwave-safe bowl

Microwave

String and a pencil (optional)

What to do:

1 Mix 2 tablespoons of sugar with 1 tablespoon of water in the bowl.

2 Microwave for 15 to 30 seconds, or until the sugar dissolves. **(Caution: hot!)**

3 **Optional:** Tie a short piece of string to a pencil, and lay the pencil over the bowl so that the string dangles in the water. The crystals that form on the string will be easier to see.

4 Wait for several days and watch for crystals.

What's happening:

When table sugar (sucrose) dissolves in water, the sucrose molecules separate and mix with the water. As the water evaporates, the sucrose molecules get closer to each other, and lock together to form crystals.

Growing sugar crystals.

Sugar crystals on a string.

CANDY CRYSTALS

Time: About 1 week

Skill Level: Get a grown-up

Some kinds of candy are made almost completely from sucrose (table sugar). Can you turn these candies into crystals?

What you need:

Altoids or mint Life Savers (crushed)

Water

Small microwave-safe bowl

Microwave

String and a pencil (optional)

What to do:

1. Mix 2 tablespoons of crushed candy with 1 tablespoon of water in the bowl.

2. Microwave 15 to 30 seconds, or until the powder dissolves. **(Caution: hot!)**
   Optional: Tie a short piece of string to a pencil, and lay the pencil over the bowl so that the string dangles in the water. The crystals that form on the string will be easier to see.

3. Wait several days and watch for crystals.

What's happening:

Mint Altoids and Life Savers are made mostly from sucrose, the kind of sugar you find in your kitchen. When the candy dissolves, the sucrose molecules separate and mix with the water. As the water evaporates, the sucrose molecules get closer to each other and lock together to form crystals.

Pea-size sugar crystal made from Altoids.

m o r e f u n

If you taste the crystals, you'll be surprised to find that they aren't as minty as the original mints. When the flavor molecules bump into the growing sugar crystals, they don't stick together very well. Eventually the flavor molecules are replaced by sugar molecules, which lock onto the crystal much better. This makes the crystals taste like plain sugar rather than mint.

DEXTROSE CRYSTALS

Time: 2 to 5 days

Skill Level: Get a grown-up

You can make crystals out of candy made mostly from sucrose (table sugar). Can you make crystals from any other kind of candy?

What you need:

8 Pixy Sticks or 2 small rolls of Smarties (crushed)

Hot water

Small microwave-safe bowl

Microwave

String and a pencil (optional)

What to do:

1. Mix the powder from the Pixy Stix or Smarties (about 1 tablespoon) with 1 tablespoon of hot water in the bowl.
2. Microwave for 15 to 30 seconds, or until the powder dissolves. **(Caution: hot!)** **Optional:** Tie a short piece of string to a pencil, and lay the pencil over the bowl so that the string dangles in the water. The crystals that form on the string will be easier to see.
3. Wait several days and watch for crystals.

What's happening:

Pixy Sticks and Smarties are made from a kind of sugar called dextrose (glucose). This kind of sugar also forms crystals. You might notice that these crystals don't look like table sugar (sucrose) crystals. Sucrose molecules and dextrose molecules look different, and they fit together in different ways. So sucrose crystals and dextrose crystals also look different.

Why do the crystals "crawl" up the side of the bowl? When the dextrose molecules start to crystallize, the first crystals form at the edge of the bowl. The dextrose water is attracted to these crystals. It seeps up into them, just as water seeps up the cotton candy in the Defying Gravity with Cotton Candy Slime experiment on page 116. When the water dries, the leftover dextrose forms new crystals on top of the old ones, making a crystal formation that looks ready to explode out of the bowl.

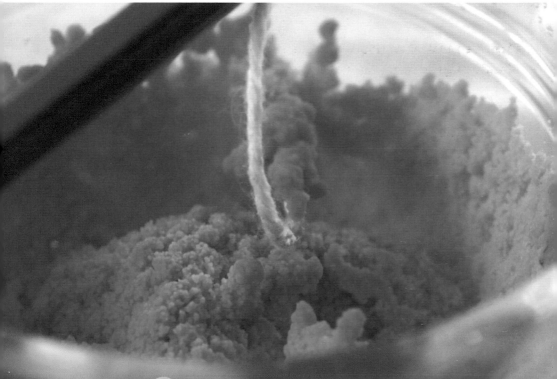

Pixy Stix crystals.

Although the crystals have formed, there's still water mixed with them. Weigh your crystal bowl every day to see how much water has evaporated.

When the crystals are completely dry, smash them with a spoon and use the powder for the Candy Water Cooler experiment on page 104.

THE NO-CRYSTAL CANDY

Time: 1 week

Skill Level: Get a grown-up

Candy made with table sugar or dextrose will form crystals. Can you make crystals with every kind of candy?

What you need:

Hard candy that contains corn syrup, such as a lollipop or Jolly Rancher

Hot water

Small microwave-safe bowl

Microwave

What to do:

1. Crush the hard candy.
2. Mix 2 tablespoons of the candy with 1 tablespoon of hot water in the bowl.
3. Microwave for 30 seconds, or until the candy dissolves. **(Caution: hot!)** Stir, and remove any lumps that won't dissolve.
4. Wait for several days, up to 1 week. Your solution should thicken without forming crystals.

What's happening:

Crystals can make candy grainy, so some kinds of candy must be made without crystals. Because of this, candy makers often add corn syrup. The different molecules in corn syrup don't lock together, so the corn syrup prevents crystals from forming.

Will dissolved Jolly
Ranchers ever
form crystals?

Some kinds of candy are sticky. Some aren't. What's the difference? And what can you do with sticky candy?

In this chapter, you'll test candy for stickiness. You'll learn why some kinds of candy are stickier than others. Then you'll learn how to make candy stickier—or how to unsticky it.

chapter 9

STICKY

STICKY TEST

Time: 5 minutes

Skill Level: Easy

You know some candies are sticky. Just how sticky are they?

What you need:

Several blocks of chewy candy, such as Starburst, Tootsie Rolls, taffy, or Laffy Taffy

Small round candies, such as Smarties or SweeTARTS

What to do:

1 Knead each chewy candy with your fingers until it is pliable.

2 Try to make a car by attaching round candy wheels to the chewy candy. Which chewy candy is stickiest?

What's happening:

Candy stickiness depends on many things. How warm is it? How much water is in it? How much oil is in it? Are there tiny air bubbles inside to make it soft? (A piece of taffy without air mixed in would be as hard as a Jolly Rancher.)

Why does candy stickiness matter? Because sticky candy contributes to cavities. If it gets stuck in your teeth, it feeds the bacteria that cause cavities. The longer it sits there, the more damage it does.

Sticky candy also damages braces. The acid made by cavity-causing bacteria eats away the glue that holds braces on your teeth. If the sticky candy sticks on braces while you're chewing, it can loosen them or even pull them off. This is why orthodontists tell kids with braces to avoid sticky candy.

Which sticky candy makes the best car?

What can you make with your sticky candy?

Make sculptures or statues with your sticky candy. What kind of candy works best for this? How high can you build? How long does your sticky sculpture stand up?

EVEN STICKIER

Time: 1 week

Skill Level: Easy

You can make some candy sticky by adding water. Can you make candy sticky without adding water?*

What you need:

Assorted candy that contains corn syrup, such as Laffy Taffy, Tootsie Rolls, Starburst, Jolly Rancher, or starlight peppermints (use 2 pieces of each kind)

Plate

Paper bag (optional)

What to do:

1. Unwrap one piece of each kind of candy. Leave the other piece wrapped.
2. Place all of the candies on the plate. (You may want to hide the plate under a paper bag or on a shelf so nobody eats the experiment.)
3. After 1 week, test the unwrapped candy. Is it stickier? Did it stick to the plate?
4. Unwrap the remaining candy and compare it to the candy on the plate. Which is stickier?

What's happening:

Sugar absorbs water. Even table sugar absorbs water from the atmosphere—that's what makes it sticky enough to form sugar lumps.

Candy made with corn syrup absorbs even more water than table sugar. The molecules in corn syrup candy aren't locked into stable crystals. This means they're more likely to stick to other molecules, including the water molecules in the air. The candy absorbs water from the atmosphere, making it stickier. So, if you live in a very dry climate, this experiment may not work well.

Yellow Laffy Taffy is sticky after sitting unwrapped for a week.

Candy that absorbs moisture from the surrounding air is **hygroscopic**.

more fun

Do you have any leftover old candy? Unwrap it and see how sticky it is. Candy made from corn syrup, like taffy or Jolly Ranchers, can turn sticky and gooey over time because it absorbs water from the atmosphere. But candy made from sugar crystals, like mint Life Savers, Altoids, or Smarties, doesn't absorb water and turn sticky.

*NOTE: This may not work in a dry climate.

LIFE SAVERS: STICKY OR NOT?

Time: 10 minutes

Skill Level: Easy

Some Life Savers get sticky. Some don't. What's the difference?

What you need:

Mint Life Savers

Fruit-flavored Life Savers

Small bowl of water

Plate

What to do:

1. Dip each Life Saver in the bowl of water and set it on the plate.
2. Wait for 2 to 5 minutes.
3. Touch each Life Saver. Which ones feel sticky?

What's happening:

Clasp your hands together. Now, with your hands still clasped, try to grab something else. Can you do it? Or is it easier to grab something when your hands are free?

Mint Life Savers are made from powdered sugar, or sugar crystals. Inside the crystals, the sugar molecules are locked together like clasped hands. Because they are bonded so tightly, they can't bond as well to other things. They aren't very sticky.

Fruit-flavored Life Savers are made from sugar cooked with corn syrup. The sugar molecules aren't locked together into crystals. They can bond more easily to other molecules, just as your free hand can easily grab something. This makes the candy sticky.

Which Life Saver gets stickier?

VAMPIRE MARSHMALLOWS

Time: 1 to 5 days

Skill Level: Easy

Can a marshmallow suck water out of a piece of bread?

What you need:

1 marshmallow

Half a piece of soft bread

Zip-top plastic bag

What to do:

1 Place the marshmallow and the piece of bread in the plastic bag. Seal the bag.

2 After 1 day, open the bag and feel the marshmallow. Does it feel softer and spongier? Is the bread drier? (If you don't notice a change, put the marshmallow and bread back in the bag and wait for a few more days before testing again.)

What's happening:

The corn syrup in the marshmallow makes the marshmallow absorb water. So when the water in the bread evaporates, it's absorbed by the marshmallow.

This vampire marshmallow will suck up water.

UNSTICKY IT

Time: 5 minutes

Skill Level: Easy

When you rip open a marshmallow, the inside is sticky. Can you unsticky it?

What you need:

1 marshmallow

Small bowl of water

What to do:

1. Tear open the marshmallow and touch the inside. Is it sticky?
2. Dip the marshmallow into the water.
3. Touch the marshmallow again. Is it still sticky?

What's happening:

Marshmallows are sticky because they're made from corn syrup. The different molecules in the corn syrup don't lock together as crystals, so they're more likely to stick to other things—including your finger.

When you dip the marshmallow in water, water molecules stick to the molecules in the marshmallow. Since the marshmallow molecules are already stuck to the water molecules, they won't stick to your finger.

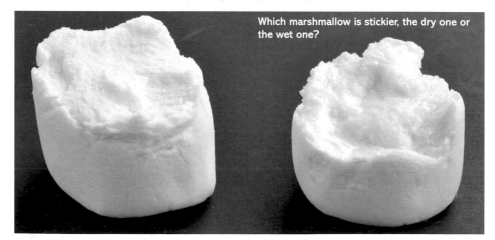

Which marshmallow is stickier, the dry one or the wet one?

INDEX

taffy
    floating and sinking experiments, 44–45, 48–49
    secret ingredient experiments, 8, 14
    stickiness experiments, 136–37
    stretchiness experiments, 86–87
    temperature experiments, 94–95, 103
temperature experiments, 92, 94–109, 114–15
tempering, 11
3 Musketeers bars, 46–47, 54–55, 70, 118
Tic Tacs, 112–13
Tootsie Pops, 122–23
Tootsie Rolls
    dissolving experiments, 110, 114–15
    floating and sinking experiments, 44–45, 48–49
    secret ingredient experiments, 8, 9, 13, 14
    stickiness experiments, 136–37, 138–39
    stretchiness experiments, 86–87
    temperature experiments, 94–95
Twix bars, 47, 53

vegetable oil, 13, 53, 57, 120–21

Warheads, 4–5, 6–7
Water
    absorption experiments, 72-73, 138-139, 141
    as candy ingredient, 68-69, 86-87, 94-95, 99, 136
Whoppers, 47, 118
Wintergreen Life Savers, 90–91, 124
wintergreen oil, 91

xylitol, 105, 108–9

Zotz candy, 5